THE OLD~FASHIONED
GARDENER

THE OLD~FASHIONED GARDENER

Lessons from the past for the gardener of today

──NIGEL COLBORN──

SPECIAL PHOTOGRAPHY BY JACQUI HURST

LORENZ BOOKS

NEW YORK • LONDON • SYDNEY • BATH

First published in the United States in 1995 by
Lorenz Books
an imprint of Anness Publishing Limited
1 Boundary Row
London SE1 8HP

ISBN 1-85967-160-8

Publisher: Joanna Lorenz
Project Editor: Jennifer Jones
Designer: Lisa Tai
Special photographer: Jacqui Hurst
Illustrator: Vana Haggerty, FLS

Printed and bound in Hong Kong

Page one: a wooden garden seat of traditional design.
Page two: an old-fashioned grass roller makes an attractive garden feature.
Page three: a colourful perennial border in a Pennsylvania garden.

CONTENTS

Introduction

Above: fan training is a traditional way to grow fruit trees, making the best use of the available wall space. Peaches require full light on a warm, sunny wall.

Detail, top right: apple blossom in spring.

Right: gardeners in the past grew a wide range of fruit and vegetables without the use of chemical fertilizers or blanket insecticides.

Gather a bouquet of fragrant roses or pluck a cluster of ripening grapes from the vine and you benefit from a programme of research and development that can be traced back several thousand years before the dawn of history. No one knows exactly how the art of gardening began, but some plants have been in cultivation for so long that their wild counterparts are not known. Horticultural skill, like the growth of civilization itself, has been erratic, with long periods of stagnation interspersed with huge leaps of achievement, but over the millennia, our gardening legacy has certainly been enriched and enhanced with each passing age.

Today, however, in spite, of rapid advances in modern technology – or perhaps because of them – we are beginning to recognize that not all recent progress has been beneficial. Pesticides, for example, have enabled us to grow high yields of fruit and vegetables that look clean and appetizing, but at what cost to the environment? And to what extent have they resulted in the development of weaker strains and varieties that depend on chemical protection rather than on natural vigour to thrive?

In some food crops, plant breeding has changed emphasis over the past half century, with genetic selection now focussed firmly on supermarket requirements, i.e. fruit and vegetables with a bright, appetizing appearance and prolonged shelf-life. But this has frequently been at the cost of flavour and wholesomeness. Modern strawberries, for example, last for days on the retailers' shelf and look luscious but have little flavour. Old varieties such as 'Late Pine' or 'Royal Sovereign' will not keep but taste delicious and are therefore ideal for private gardeners.

Some modern horticultural practices are now known to be positively harmful and many growers have turned their backs on all but the most ecology-conscious methods. Blanket insecticides that destroy virtually all invertebrate life find favour with few private gardeners these days, since they destroy beneficial species as well as pests and hence upset the natural balance, possibly creating more serious pest problems later on. Far better to adopt the approach used before we had such a battery of

An old-fashioned kitchen garden can be both productive and decorative.

stuck to many of the old methods are just as able to produce large crops of delicious vegetables and glorious displays of flowers as those who use modern methods.

Much of the old-fashioned gardening know-how is based on folklore, or on a collection of hand-me-down knowledge and experience. Some of this wisdom may, in this scientific age, sometimes seem dubious, but there is no doubt that some old customs have stuck because they still have tangible merit. Before the age of technology gardeners were, for instance, far more closely in tune with the passing of the seasons; so much of the work ran with the calender, and even today weather is surely the biggest factor in gardening anywhere in the world. It is one thing over which technology has no control and yet it holds the strongest influence over the way in which we grow our plants. It is hardly surprising therefore that nine-tenths of gardening lore relates to weather and the prediction of its effects on crops.

Mild spells in midwinter, for example, have traditionally been regarded with distrust. 'If looks green in Janiveer,' says the ancient proverb, 'twill look the worser all the year.' This suggests that growing in January – the coldest month in the Northern hemisphere – is unnatural and will debilitate plants, reducing their growth later on. In spring, on the other hand, the preoccupation has always been the need for the land to dry up enough to be workable early in the season. Hence the saying, 'A peck of March dust is worth a king's ransom'. Spring is a tense time for gardeners, compounded by the fact that around the vernal equinox the weather all over the world is at its most fickle so that in cold climates a gardener could experience a blizzard or a heatwave within a couple of days of each other.

Once the spring plants are established everyone looks to the skies for gentle rain to swell the fruit and convert the borders into a

chemical weapons and use old-fashioned good husbandry to ensure that the plants thrive.

The object of this book is to examine traditional practices, and old-fashioned plants and designs, and to see how the best of these can be applied to modern-day gardening. Some techniques, such as grafting or rooting cuttings, have always been with us and are likely to remain an important part of any gardener's list of skills. Others, such as double digging, use of organic fertilizers and composting, have tended to be abandoned in favour of easier substitutes in the form of mechanical cultivation and chemical fertilizers. And yet those gardeners who eschew space-age technology and have

The renewed interest in organic gardening has encouraged gardeners to look at the past to see how their forebears worked the land without access to a whole battery of chemical fertilizers and insecticides. In addition, gardeners everywhere – while taking advantage of modern plant breeding programmes that have developed more disease-resistant varieties, and dwarf forms that are ideal for smaller gardens – are beginning to appreciate older varieties of plants for their beauty. Many old flowers are justifiably enjoying a revival. The roses cultivated in the eighteenth and nineteenth centuries, which, having all but disappeared between the two world wars, are now widely grown and enjoyed for their gentle colours and strength of fragrance by new generations of gardeners. Old florists' flowers such as carnations and pinks with their laced markings, and auriculas with their jewel-like colours and velvet texture, are also back in vogue and make happy companions to the more modern varieties of the same genera. Many people are therefore looking again at horticultural history, not only for nostalgic reasons, but because the past has so much to offer modern gardeners.

glorious summer display. Traditionally, stormy weather in early spring was thought to augur well for growth, hence 'When April blows his horn, tis good for hay and corn.' Conditions at planting were very important too, with seed needing to be sown in crumbly soil, but young plants wanting plenty of moisture for their roots: 'This rule in gardening never forget; to sow dry and to set wet.'

Harvest too was beset with traditions, many of them still sound today. The deep freeze has taken much of the romance out of kitchen gardening, but when preserving food was more difficult it was important to maximize not only the variety of produce brought in from the garden, but also to stagger the season so that the supply was more evenly spread through the year. Some crops would therefore be allowed to grow to maturity – courgettes, or zucchini, would grow to huge marrows for winter storage, for example – others were rotated quickly so that a steady supply of such fresh greens as coleworts or lettuces could supplement the diet. But as well as using the land efficiently, this more prudent form of kitchen gardening was far more attractive visually, so that working among the vegetables was a pleasure in itself.

Budding knives, 1859

A re-creation of a medieval physic garden.

*Left: a modern flower
garden combines grasses, a
fairly recent planting idea,
with* Rosa gallica
'Versicolour', *or* 'Rosa
Mundi', *which has been
grown for at least 400 years
and is still one of the best
shrub roses in cultivation.*

THE
PRODUCTIVE
GARDEN

Gardeners of the past successfully produced bountiful crops of fresh, healthy and flavourful fruits and vegetables without resource to any of the artificial aids and chemicals relied on today by so many market gardeners. They had a greater appreciation of the importance of the soil, the climate, the seasons and better understanding of the requirements of individual plants. There are many ways in which we can learn from their methods, and achieve for ourselves magnificent and healthy organic produce grown by entirely natural methods.

The kitchen garden

Previous page: the fruits of a well-tended kitchen garden. Detail: forced rhubarb.

The gaunt foliage of the cabbage family in the kitchen garden can be relieved by interplanting of herbs. Here, lavender and parsley make a colourful border along the pathway without too much growing space being sacrificed.

There have always been amateur gardeners so absorbed with the delights of growing their own food that to have to buy any part of their produce would be an admission of failure. One of my proudest moments was an occasion when my wife and I threw a dinner party at which every scrap of food – including the roast pork and even the flour for the freshly baked bread – came entirely from our own resources. But I also remember the aching back!

The main function of the period kitchen garden was always, first and foremost, to provide food – and lots of it. In earlier times, of course, most people had to rely on the food they grew themselves. If they lived in the city, they relied on the numerous market gardens that inevitably sprang up wherever there were concentrations of population. (The French in

particular excelled at intensive market gardening, and used frame lights, bell glasses and cloches extensively.) For the rich, the kitchen garden was the province of the head gardener and his team of assistants. The professional gardener working for the large private house placed great emphasis on producing not only food of the highest quality, but also many unseasonal delicacies. By the eighteenth century, for example, a well-managed kitchen garden would supply strawberries for Easter, tender new potatoes in late winter, orchard fruit harvested from specially forced container-grown trees in late spring, and so on.

During the World Wars and the early post-war shortages in Europe, home-grown food was again a necessity, helping to eke out the meagre food rations. It became acceptable for cabbages and Brussels sprouts to grow in borders which lined the garden path to the front door. Gardens were productive, but in many cases were not much uglier for that. Indeed, it might even be argued that a well-tended food garden, even if it does front the house, can look much more attractive than an ill-conceived and fussy mixed planting of gaudy bedding flowers.

Later, during the 1960s and 1970s, because of low-priced fruit and vegetables, kitchen gardens lost their appeal and fewer gardeners grew their own food. In recent years, however, there has been a resurgence of interest in home food production as concerns over health issues have grown. Pesticides are used extensively in commercial market gardening, yet little is

Whether as part of a kitchen garden or purely as part of an ornamental garden, espalier apples have, for centuries, been used to make attractive boundaries.

known about their long term effect on both the environment and the human body. Many farmers also rely on chemical fertilizers. Their widespread use is testimony to their effectiveness, but again in the long-term they could lead to a depletion of organic matter in the soil and the organisms that live in it, which in turn affects the vitality and robustness of growing plants. There is no simple answer to this problem when applied on a commercial scale, but the amateur gardener can do much to minimize the need for pesticides and other chemicals in the garden. And, as anyone knows who has tried freshly picked produce which has travelled no further than from the bottom of the garden, there's nothing to beat the taste of home-grown food.

Today the average garden plot is considerably smaller than it was even fifty years ago.

Yet, ironically, people expect a great deal more from their gardens nowadays than formerly. This puts the ground under considerable pressure from every point of view, but it is especially difficult when it comes to growing vegetables. Thoughtful design and layout can certainly help here, however, together with a number of natural techniques for growing and forcing vegetables – old-fashioned methods first used by those French market gardeners in the seventeenth century.

Design and layout

Kitchen gardens are not just expected to be productive these days, they're also expected to look good. A carefully considered design in the kitchen garden also has a practical advantage. It will help you to plan your vegetable growing so

Garden spade

that you benefit from crops throughout the year. A clear layout will also help you to decide what varieties to grow and how much seed you will need. Most of the designs for kitchen gardens in the past were clearly laid out with such things in mind, and also provided scope for ornamental features.

THE MONASTIC VEGETABLE GARDEN

The layout favoured by medieval monks made the most of limited space by using small, square or rectangular raised beds edged with elm wood planks and divided by narrow paths, creating a neat, orderly and geometric design. This is, in fact, also an excellent formula for the small modern garden.

This simple but attractive design allowed the monks to break up a planting scheme in a number of useful ways. They could grow as many or as few varieties as they liked within the given space, and in clearly defined areas. For the modern gardener, this makes the management of crop rotation (see page 30) much easier. The small beds allowed the monks to tend their plants from the path without treading on the soil, minimizing compaction and enabling plants to be grown in blocks instead of rows. The fashion in recent times has

Medieval gardens often featured bowers or arbours on which vines could be trained. Nowadays, lightweight modern materials allow such structures to be made at relatively low cost.

been to grow vegetables in long rows, but growing vegetables tightly together in raised, deep beds will not take up more space and allows for a stronger design element to be introduced into the garden.

The monks did in fact include such features as pergolas and arbours in their vegetable gardens, and these would not look out of place, therefore, in a garden which adopted the monastic design. The monks used the pergolas as supports for climbers such as vines, but it must have been pleasant, too, to walk through a leafy canopy on a hot summer's day. Undoubtedly trelliswork arbours were positioned to enjoy the best view of the vegetable garden!

THE COTTAGE KITCHEN GARDEN

In contrast to the monastic layout, the cottage gardener happily combined vegetables and flowers in a single plot of land, the one often spilling into the other. Most people today are more familiar with the purely ornamental cottage garden (see page 62), but the productive cottage garden offers the modern gardener some good ideas too, particularly for those who enjoy flowers but do not want to sacrifice valuable crop space.

Although cottage gardens have been around for hundreds of years in one form or another, it wasn't until the early part of the nineteenth century that they took on an identifiable form. One man responsible for this was the great Scottish gardener and philanthropist, John Claudius Loudon, who helped to promote the idea of model estates with model cottages for the estate workers. He suggested that each small but elegantly designed cottage should have a plot roomy enough to allow the inhabitants to raise their own food, adequate space for drying clothes and even space for some form of ornamental gardening.

From this emerged a design formula that has stood the test of time and proved extremely

A careful selection and arrangement of food crops helps to make the cottage kitchen garden more productive and ornamental. The beans in the background are as beautiful in flower as they are later fruitful. The spinach, lining the path, can be cut repeatedly for a long-lasting supply.

“ CERTAIN IT IS THAT THE KITCHEN GARDEN REQUIRES THE WARMEST SITUATION AND THE RICHEST SOIL THAT A GARDEN DOES, … ”

Stephen Switzer, 1727

with neat rows of vegetables and soft fruits. In the latter, the small front garden was usually left to hardy perennials and annuals which would be encouraged to grow in plentiful profusion, while the back garden was devoted to growing fruit and vegetables. The flowers were often densely planted to form an attractive and uncontrived jumble of shapes and colour, and needed little weeding or staking.

This is not an approach for the very small garden, where the combination of formal and informal would be overwhelming and unwieldy. Nor, perhaps, is it one for the heart of a city (though it has been known), but it would work well for most other medium-sized modern gardens. It uses space economically and makes room for prettiness. The beauty of the cottage garden is that almost anything goes, in fact that is part of its charm. Its inventive occupants were never afraid to use new material or ideas (greenhouses, for example, were taken up enthusiastically by cottagers as cheap ones became available). In a formal garden, a fruit tree grown in a hedgerow on the perimeter of the garden would look out of place, but in a cottage garden it was quite a common feature and looks perfectly at home, as well as being an excellent tip for saving space. In the traditional cottage garden nothing is left if it can be used for something else too. On the cottages of old, the walls provided support for wall fruits. The area outside the kitchen door would be used for growing herbs, where they would be close to hand for picking and throwing into the pot.

workable for generations of cottagers. It is certainly worth considering for the modern garden. There were two basic approaches, to suit either a garden situated at the front of the house, or one with a small front garden and a larger plot at the rear. In the former, flowers were planted either side of the central path that ran from the gate to the front door. The rest of the available space was then taken up

Rhubarb chard, growing here in the potager at Château Villandry in France, is a useful vegetable in the potager, since individual leaves and stems can be harvested as required, allowing the plant to continue to grow and to create a display.

THE POTAGER

Ornamental kitchen gardening was very popular in France in the fifteenth and sixteenth centuries, and the reconstruction and continued upkeep of a decorative *jardin potager* at Château Villandry in France by the Carvello family is justifiably renowned. There has been a revival of interest in recent years in this ornamental approach to vegetable growing. Succession (see page 22) is an important feature of such a potager, since it is supposed to look attractive and give an impression of fullness for most of the year.

But its beauty does not just lie in the skilful planting and harvesting of vegetables – seen in winter under a covering of snow, Villandry is equally stunning. This is because it also relies on a number of permanent features for effect, and these can give the gardener of even a small plot and less ambitious aims plenty of ideas.

The potager at Villandry is a parterre made up of nine square compartments. Each compartment is surrounded by low trelliswork,

This ingenious homemade gadget is useful for marking out parallel rows of vegetables. In the old-fashioned potager, symmetry not only ensures a fine display, it also guarantees optimum use of land.

which provides the perfect support for training dwarf fruit trees. Within each compartment the beds form geometric shapes – crosses, 'L' shapes, rectangles, squares and so on – outlined in dwarf box. These are planted with a wide range of vegetables in such a way as to create maximum impact in terms of colour and texture. Fresh cabbages look wonderful contrasting their brash, glaucous foliage with ferny carrot leaves, for example, and silvery-green plants as handsome as globe artichokes would grace their surroundings anywhere. The red form of Swiss chard makes a stirring display with its bright green foliage and deep red stems. There are also ornamental cabbages which are edible as well as beautiful and their close relative, the seakale, whose blue-green foliage and honey-scented white flowers make it a lovely perennial that is delicious blanched in winter. Among climbing beans, herbaceous climbers such as nasturtiums or sweet peas would add colour and fragrance.

Flowers have their place, too. Rose trees are planted in some of the beds, and the beds on the perimeter of each compartment are also planted with flowers. At the centre of each compartment is a stone pillar topped with an urn filled with flowers. Where four compartments meet in the centre aisle, in each case there is a small fountain and each corner is given a trelliswork arbour facing out.

Such garden ornaments and features give the garden form and character, while providing many of the planting benefits of the monastic garden (see page 14). Even a small modern garden would benefit from such a design. It could, for example, consist of one simple parterre, outlined in either low trelliswork or dwarf box, at the centre of which could stand a pillar, geometric form or even a statue. A simple seat would be the easiest alternative to an arbour, or a basic arbour could be made from wooden posts and used to grow climbers.

Cast iron hand glass, 1859

THE COLONIAL KITCHEN GARDEN

In Colonial America, the kitchen garden often took pride of place, the most popular layout being the 'quadrant' design. This is still an efficient way to grow food crops in a small space, and the simple but effective layout would be easy to adopt and maintain.

The design consisted of a neatly fenced-in square situated near the house. The border running along the inside of the fence would usually be planted with self-perpetuating herbs and vegetables such as horseradish, asparagus, chives and mints. The centre of the square, which consisted of four smaller square-shaped beds divided by narrow paths, was devoted to annual herbs and vegetables. These included potatoes, beans, onions, cabbages, and useful culinary herbs such as basil and parsley.

As with monastery gardens, these crop beds would have been raised and liberally manured for maximum yield. The design is perfect for the four-year rotation plan (see page 30).

THE KITCHEN GARDEN

The classic walled kitchen garden of the nineteenth century was also based on the cruciform plan, with a deep border running the length of the walls and four large beds in the centre with paths laid out to provide easy access to all parts of the garden.

The Gardener's Assistant, which was published in 1859, contains advice typical of the time which the modern gardener would also do well to heed. It recommends that soil in the kitchen garden either be level 'but admitting of effectual drainage' or have a gentle slope to the south, south-east or south-west 'so that it may be more sheltered from northerly winds; whilst at the same time, its inclination admits of the sun's rays acting with greater effect.'

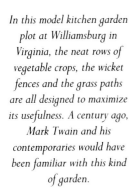

In this model kitchen garden plot at Williamsburg in Virginia, the neat rows of vegetable crops, the wicket fences and the grass paths are all designed to maximize its usefulness. A century ago, Mark Twain and his contemporaries would have been familiar with this kind of garden.

Nineteenth-century gardeners were very keen on making the most of the sun on their walls in order to ripen their fruits to perfection. Again, *The Gardener's Assistant* offers careful observations and calculations to make the most of this sometimes elusive commodity in the Northern hemisphere. Few gardeners today would want to go to the lengths they suggest, but it does make interesting reading and provides some useful indicators on how to get the most from fruit trees trained against walls, fences or free-standing. In the warmer parts of Britain (and most of Europe), it recommends that the wall at the northern end of the kitchen garden should face the sun at eleven a.m., and the walls on the east and west sides should run parallel to each other, and at right angles to the north and south walls. In colder climates, the wall on the north side should face direct south, again with east and west at right angles to it; but if the south wall is of limited extent, the walls should form a rhombus. Where the hottest aspect is necessary to ripen the peach and nectarine, the wall on the northern side should face the sun at one p.m., and the walls on the eastern and western sides should then form a rhomboid.

The Gardener's Assistant suggests that a square walled garden is the most economic to build (there is less wall than with other shapes), but that if you want more wall, and more fruit, then the rhomboid or rhombus is recommended. But above all it recommends the parallelogram 'of which,' it says, 'the length is as five to three in breadth.'

The authors put forward a note of caution as far as walls are concerned, however. 'Walls afford good shelter so long as there is but little wind, and that steady; but when it is otherwise, it eddies round the inside of the walls, and if cold, it produces far more injurious effects on the vegetation which it there meets, than it does on that which is entirely on the open

ground, and not subjected to temporary excitements.' The solution, they suggest, is to plant trees outside the walled garden in the direction of the worst of the wind. On the north and north-east sides the trees can be quite close to the wall (about 18 m/60 ft), but on the south, west and east sides the trees should be planted further away so as not to obscure the light reaching the produce on the other side.

A working kitchen garden

Since vegetable planting is invariably of a fussy nature, the design for a kitchen garden should be kept as simple as possible, particularly where the area employed is small, for example in the American Colonial style (see page 17). It is essential that all parts of the garden are readily accessible for cultivating the soil, harvesting, weeding and so on.

Whatever design you choose, make sure the

Left: sieves, riddles, dibbers and a watering can — all stock in trade for the kitchen gardener who would want to grade his composts according to particle size and to make holes for his transplants quickly without bending his back too much.

Right: in an ornamental kitchen garden, colour combinations, though incidental to the main objective of raising food, are nonetheless important. Whether by design or accident, these dark-leaved brassicas make a fine contrast with the lettuces and beans.

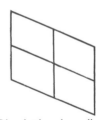

Rhomboid garden walls

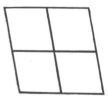

Rhombus garden walls

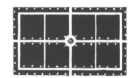

Kitchen garden design, 1859

Melons are among the earliest of cultivated plants. They require hot weather to mature and develop their sweetness. In cold climates, the most effective way to grow them is to start them off in a hotbed.

Rain gauge

area is a sunny site that drains well. It should also be sheltered as much as possible from the prevailing wind. A walled garden would be very expensive, but a trelliswork fence would provide an effective windbreak. Alternatively, hedging (see page 93) is another option, although not if you are short of space.

When productivity is the main objective in a small space, it's best not to overdo the number of low hedges, dividing pathways and central features, all of which can erode away the amount of space available for cultivation. Nevertheless, the plot can still achieve considerable charm if the production is arranged in an orderly fashion and by building in a feature or two that will add to the overall interest.

The main path can be made into an attractive feature. *The Gardener's Assistant* spends some time on the problem of paths. 'When we take into consideration the cost of gravel walks in the first instance, and the subsequent expense of rolling, weeding, turning, and occasional renewing, it is questionable whether stone

paving would not prove cheaper than gravel in the long run.' This holds true today, but instead of stone you could try brick. The path should be wide enough to walk on comfortably, but not so wide as to rob valuable growing space. Any secondary paths should be kept as narrow as possible to avoid wasting space. Such paths could be furnished with a straw mulch, a thin gravel skim or consist of little more than compacted earth. Alternatively, they could be made 'movable' by using planks of wood. Paying attention to these details will ensure a maximum growing area.

Non-essential but nonetheless extremely useful items would include a compost bay, which can be hidden from view by hedging or a trellis screen or fence, preferably with two divisions so one side can be making while the other is supplying finished product (see page 148). If birds are a problem and you want to grow soft fruit, a fruit cage would be useful. To extend the season and widen your scope, a set of cold frames (see page 117) would also be a

A hotbed is the cheapest source of energy. Heat is produced by bacteria rotting fresh dung and conserved by the covering frame. Seeds or young plants should be placed in containers on the layer of soil covering the dung.

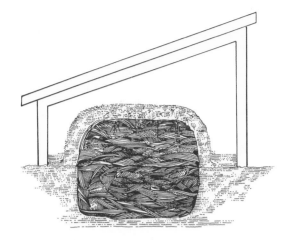

handy addition in the small kitchen garden. Cloches or hand lights (see page 118) were also widely used in the eighteenth and nineteenth centuries, providing localized protection to newly set out plants and also warming up the soil prior to handling. Modern cloches and plastic sheeting do the same job but not so well, and far less elegantly.

A greenhouse (see page 115) would make a delightful feature and could double your productivity. It will certainly treble your enjoyment! Propagation is so much easier if you can protect young seedlings, and even an unheated greenhouse will extend the growing season and increase productivity enormously. It will also add greatly to your scope in the flower garden, particularly when it comes to raising frost-tender plants in early spring. Gardeners in the nineteenth century made much use of harnessing the heat given off by bacteria as they decomposed dung. This was achieved by building a hotbed – which is a cheap source of energy, and worth trying if you can get hold of enough fresh animal manure.

Waterbarrow

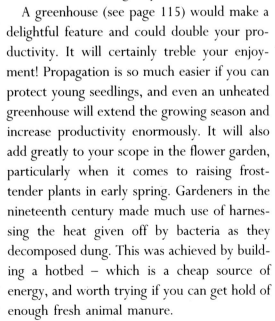

Wheelbarrow

Garden watering engine

The traditional hotbed or frame is seldom employed these days, which is a pity, because a more environmentally friendly means of providing lasting warmth to the soil is hard to imagine. *The Annals of Horticulture* (1846) describes the whole involved and rather messy procedure in graphic detail. Fresh horse dung was heaped up, and allowed to become hot in the heap. It was then turned over, sprinkled with water if it showed a tendency to dry out, and heaped up to heat again. The hot frame – a movable object – was then laid on the ground as a marker for its final position, the corners marked with four stakes and the frame then removed again. The dung was carefully piled and gently compressed in the exact shape of the frame to a depth of 90 cm (3 ft) to 107 cm (3½ ft). The frame was then fitted over the dung and a long stick thrust through the side into the heap so that it could be pulled out from time to time in order to gauge the temperature.

The heap was then left to settle down for a few days before a layer of good loam, about 7.5 cm (3 in) thick, was spread over the surface of the hotbed. The result was a steady emission of bottom heat as bacteria in the dung carried out the process of decomposition. Seeds were sown, not directly into the soil, but in pans or trays, which were then laid on top. The glass

" ...*T*HE GARDEN SHOULD BE SO NEAR TO THE MANSION AS TO BE CONVENIENTLY ACCESSIBLE ON FOOT ... WHILE IT SHOULD BE SO DISTANT AS TO AVOID THE POSSIBILITY OF OFFENCE ARISING FROM THE NECESSARY GARDENING OPERATIONS, AND THE RESORT OF WORKMEN. "

Neil's *Fruit, Flower, and Kitchen Gardens*, 1900s

Marigolds are believed to exude insecticidal material from their roots which, when absorbed by the neighbouring tomato plants, could help to reduce white fly infestations. Whether this works is open to debate, but in any case the colourful plant combination looks delightful.

Sowing in succession ensures a steady supply of truly fresh produce. The radishes in the foreground were probably sown less than a fortnight before; the lettuces are about six weeks old.

lid of the frame could be lifted for ventilation during the day or left closed for the warmth and safety of the seedlings overnight. There is no reason why such a hotbed should not be built today. Apart from the aesthetic considerations, the only restraint would be the availability of fresh horse dung!

A note on companion planting This is really a modern concept beloved of new-age organic gardeners. It is not based on science or observation, but on folklore heavily spiced with romance. The idea is that some plants are happiest growing with certain neighbours, and that the impact of pest damage can be minimized and plant performance maximized if certain plant associations are adhered to.

Garlic, for instance, is said to help roses grow well, and onions, with their distracting smell, are thought to keep carrot fly away from carrots. Nasturtiums are said to lure aphids, while aubergines (eggplants) lure flea beetles. Marigolds are said to prevent aphids and whitefly from attacking tomatoes when they are planted alongside. The reality is that there are so many variable factors affecting how plants grow that it is impossible either to prove or disprove a great many of these theories. Again, French marigolds are believed to distract cabbage white butterflies and prevent them from laying eggs on brassicas planted nearby – but I need to add that this never worked for me . . . however, the flowers look so pretty that no harm is done by trying.

VEGETABLES IN SUCCESSION

Leaf through any nineteenth-century gardening book and the advice to sow vegetable seeds is repeated for almost every month. Practical tips in the 1846 issues of the *Horticultural Magazine* suggest that salad plants should be sown at monthly intervals throughout the growing season. In summer, lettuce and cucumbers predominate, but in winter, corn salad, endive and

salad rape can take their places. A greenhouse enables growers to sow almost all year round, but there are plenty of rugged plants such as land cress and sorrel which provide a 'bite' of greenery through the dark days of winter as well as a wealth of greenery in summer.

With adequate planning it was not difficult to ensure a succession of harvests during the growing season. In modern gardens this is desirable too, but most of us have little choice but to harvest more crop from less land. One distinct advantage we do have over our forebears is that modern vegetable and salad hybrids tend to yield more generously and are more disease-resistant than early counterparts.

Root vegetables, aside from the bulk of the crop which is sown in early spring for autumn

In an ornamental kitchen garden or a potager, harvesting is done piecemeal and care must be taken to minimize disturbance to other parts of the plot. As soon as one crop is removed, the ground should be prepared to receive its next occupant.

The practice of succession and continuity is exemplified in this New England vegetable garden. Earlier crops have been replaced by a mid-season crop of cos lettuce which will ripen beside the scarlet runner beans and the cucumbers.

harvest, can be successfully sown at other times of year to provide tender young roots. Carrots and beets, for example, can be sown throughout spring and early summer, almost up to the longest day, and will produce a succession of tender, baby crops. Likewise, peas can be sown in three main stages during spring to ensure a continuous crop of fresh, sweet-flavoured pods. Autumn is the season in which to sow the following year's first broad beans (except in the most severe winter areas), since overwintered plants will be ready for harvest by about mid-spring.

Perennial vegetables, such as asparagus and Jerusalem artichokes, crop heavily in season but cannot be persuaded to perform beyond a week or two outside their allotted time. Nineteenth-century gardeners were fond of forcing asparagus to sprout early by growing it in mounded beds, heaped, in spring, with raw, compacted manure which then acted like a hotbed and generated heat as it rotted.

Ensuring a succession of crops for harvesting during winter is less easy. Most pulses – peas, beans, lentils – are summer crops. Such members of the tomato family as peppers, aubergines (eggplants), chillis and potatoes are frost-tender and so die at the onset of autumn. But the mainstay of the medieval winter garden was what the ancients called coleworts and what we know as brassicas. By the nineteenth century, 'colewort' had come to refer specifically to young cabbage plants which were eaten before a heart had formed. 'As they are always eaten young,' states Mrs Loudon in *Gardening for Ladies* (1846), 'they need not be planted more than ten or twelve inches [25–30 cm] apart every way; and, when they are gathered, the stalks are pulled up and thrown away.' But, with restricted space, it is more efficient these days to adopt a cut-and-come-again policy and grow large kales or broccolis from which you can snip young green shoots on a regular basis throughout the autumn and spring, and during the winter in mild climates.

Brussels sprouts, in Mrs Loudon's day, were quite different from the tight little buttons we enjoy today. She describes them as a kind of Savoy cabbage: 'The plants first produce a small Savoy in an elongated stalk, and, when this is cut off, the long stalk throws out a number of little wrinkled-leaved cabbages from its sides,

66 ... *I*T MUST BE NOTED AS A VERY GREAT ERROR IN MOST GARDENS, AND WHICH CAUSES THEM THAT THEY ARE NOT STOCK'D WITH HALF THAT VARIETY AS THEY OUGHT, THAT GARDINERS GENERALLY SOW OR PLANT MORE OF A KIND THAN IS USEFUL, WHICH IS THE OCCASION THAT HE HAS NOT ROOM FOR SO MANY THINGS, NOR TO COME IN SO MANY DIFFERENT SEASONS AS OTHERWISE HE MIGHT. 99

Stephen Switzer, 1727

Left: with their shapely lines, nineteenth-century rhubarb-forcing pots have become valuable ornaments in their own right. To make them effective, they must be put over the rhubarb or seakale just before growth begins.

Below: in the early nineteenth century, Mrs Loudon knew that leeks performed best if planted in deep holes which were filled with water and then left open. These leeks will mature after the sweet peas in the background have finished flowering and can be left in the ground until required for the pot.

which are the brussels sprouts.' She goes on to explain that the seed is generally procured from Brussels and that their culture is the same as for Savoy cabbage, recommending that they are grown no more than 30 cm (12 in) apart. Clearly, these were much smaller plants than our modern versions. One point she does make which is as true today as ever is this: 'Both Savoys and Brussels Sprouts are considered much better if not cut till there has been some frost upon them; and they are consequently of great value as winter vegetables.'

Earlier varieties of Brussels sprouts were excellent for private gardeners, because they tended to mature slowly, over a long period, enabling one to pick them as required through-out winter. Modern F1 hybrids have been bred for commercial growers, who prefer the whole crop to be ready at once so that they can pick the lot in one go with mechanical harvesters. For home-grown purposes, standard varieties such as 'Groninger Stiekema No 1' are a wise choice since, like earlier kinds, they crop from early autumn until spring. For the ornamental kitchen garden, there are red-leaved sprouts, known as 'Rubin', whose flavour is more nutty and whose crop is spread through the season.

Leeks are another faithful standby, sitting steadfastly in the ground through autumn and winter, barely growing but not deteriorating as long as the weather stays cold.

FORCING

In winter and spring, certain plants can be tricked into premature growth by applying heat. Rhubarb, for example, can be encouraged to produce tender young stems which are not nearly so tart as the coarser, later growths, simply by placing an object over the plants to warm them and darken them. Nineteenth-century gardeners used attractive terracotta devices shaped like chimney pots with removable lids so that the stems were drawn rapidly

upwards towards the light. Generally speaking, the more quickly a plant grows, the softer and therefore the more tender its tissues will be. The same effect can be achieved using anything that blocks out the light, from an inverted garbage can to a custom-made forcer, but it has to be said that the old terracotta articles were much more attractive.

Seakale (*Crambe maritima*) was another favourite for forcing. During the 1780s Doctor Lettsom, a physician who was also a gifted botanist, spotted the plant growing on the southern coast of England and soon found out that the local fishermen and labourers used its succulent young shoots to supplement their meagre diets. He sent plants to William Curtis, founder of the *Botanical Magazine*, who multiplied them in his nursery at Lambeth Marsh near London. By the middle of the next century Mrs Loudon (1846) was able to write that this 'long-neglected British plant, which for so many years was only eaten by the poorest fishermen, became our highly prized and much esteemed sea-kale, which is now so great a favourite at the tables of the rich.'

The traditional forcing procedure is rather disgusting, by modern standards, since it uses the decay of dung as a source of natural heat. Year-old plants are transplanted into fertile raised beds, much as with asparagus, and any flower stems on the seakale removed, as these tend to weaken the roots. In their second year, the beds are covered with sand and forcing pots – not dissimilar to rhubarb forcers – are placed over each plant. Fresh horse dung is then placed over the whole bed to a depth of 50 cm (20 in). The heat generated then encourages the kale, even in late winter, to throw up succulent young shoots which have a delicate, nutty flavour. If you find the idea of all that dung makes you squeamish, just remember that the plants are separated from it by clay pots and that horses are basically clean feeders!

Top: as an alternative to earthing up, paper or cardboard collars can be used to keep out the light when blanching celery.

Above: chicory can also be forced in winter to provide fresh leafy material. In complete darkness and with a little warmth, the roots will produce large rosette buds within a few weeks.

BLANCHING

Blanching is a slightly different technique from forcing in that the object is to whiten, and so tenderize and sweeten, the plant's edible parts. Plants which are naturally bitter when grown in full light are usually more palatable if they have been etiolated, that is to say, grown in poor light conditions. With the result of modern breeding programmes, it has been possible to raise celery without the need to blanch. But none of the so-called 'self-blanching' varieties has anything like the flavour or texture of the older kinds. To blanch celery, wrap it around with paper and then 'earth it up' by heaping the soil up, burying the wrapped celery almost to the tops of the leaves.

Endive, a salad plant sown during the middle of summer, has to be blanched to assuage its bitterness, but this is a skilled job, because few salad crops rot more easily than the tangled, lacy leaves of the endive. A hundred or more years ago, the traditional method, which was popular in France, where the crop was most widely grown, was simply to tie the outer leaves tightly round the inner ones using string or osier twigs. If this operation was not carried out in dry weather, however, the massed foliage soon rotted. A much easier alternative is to stand an inverted flower pot over each endive as it matures, with a cover over the drainage hole to prevent almost all light from getting in. The plants should then be ready within a couple of weeks, but since rotting can still be a problem, it is a good idea to blanch only a few endives at a time.

One of the crispest winter salad vegetables is harvested as a result of a combination of both blanching and forcing. Chicory, or succory as it used to be called, is a plant of the daisy family. It has pretty, sky-blue flowers and large tap roots which store food. The technique for producing salad chicory is simple. The plants are grown from seed outdoors for a season before the fleshy roots are lifted in autumn, then transferred to boxes or trays and covered with moist sand or a mixture of sand and peat, leaving the tops of the roots just exposed. Place in a cool cellar, and, during the latter half of winter, these roots will throw a series of large buds or shoots which can be cut off and used in a salad. As long as they are grown in absolute darkness, these will be a creamy white, with just enough of a hint of bitterness to make them a flavoursome addition to the salad.

A HERB AND SALAD GARDEN

If space is severely limited, even if there is insufficient room for serious food production, it may still be possible to raise herbs and small quantities of salad material for the kitchen. Such bulk vegetables as cabbages, potatoes and pumpkins take up lots of space and are cheap and easy to buy at the supermarket. Truly fresh aromatic herbs, crisp salad items and fresh green garnishes are much harder to find in the shops, tend to be expensive, and can be grown in a very small space.

Herbs Many of the easiest pot herbs make glorious garden plants, worth growing just for their looks. Everyone knows how pretty rosemary and lavender can be, but there are so many others, all of them steeped in history. Coriander, besides its bewitching aroma, is a refined annual with soft feathery foliage and pink lacy flowers, and is a simple herb to raise from seed in no more than a few square centimetres (square inches); oregano, both in plain green and its golden form, is a beautiful species, beloved of bees and butterflies; basil, an essential ingredient for Italian pesto, comes in a number of decorative forms, including one with deep purple foliage.

Monks in the Dark Ages grew their herbs in physic gardens (see page 58), mainly for medicinal purposes. In the more ornamental medieval gardens, however, a chequerboard

Above: an old-fashioned herb garden can produce far more aromatic herbs and fragrances than even a large household could possibly use, but no excuse is needed for growing such a glorious mixture of plants in such a delightful setting.

Right: this miscellany of unusual herbs includes lady's mantle, blood-veined dock and hound's-tongue, all of which were traditionally grown in physic gardens. Their medicinal value may be a thing of the past, but these plants still make attractive additions to the modern herb garden.

pattern was used to grow herbs 'for Meate or Medicine, for Use or for Delight', and this system also works well in a small modern garden. Here, paving stones are set alternately with tiny growing beds, each of which is allocated a single herb. This is useful for keeping the more rampant species such as mint or tarragon within bounds, but allows more delicate herbs such as basil to receive extra attention and, if necessary, to be grown in special soil.

Another effective design is that of the traditional American herb garden. Early settlers relied on home-grown herbs to cure a wide range of ailments, to dye clothes, to add flavourings to the pot, and to sweeten the home. Naturally, they were always grown near to the house, close to hand, and carefully nurtured. The layout consisted of a square or rectangle marked out by picket fencing and the area within divided by one or two paths leading to and around a central island, which was often

Herb gardens laid in busy patterns enable different species to be grown in special compartments. The chequerboard design (right) ensures easy access to plants for tending and gathering, but the ram's horn theme (below) allows for a stronger focal point in the centre of the design.

Many of the traditional herbs of the west originated in the Mediterranean region where aromatic species flourish in the arid landscape. Sage, especially garden forms like this purple variety, look happy among borage and parsley.

the site of a beehive – the honey from this must have been superbly scented from the many sweet herbs visited by the bees, and of course the bees would have aided pollination too. The remaining space was used for raised herb beds flanked with wooden planks; such deep contained beds would have provided better drainage and prevented the more invasive herbs from growing on to the paths.

The early Americans grew a wide range of herbs from the seeds they had brought with them from Europe, including thyme, winter and summer savory, hyssop, basil, angelica, elecampane, rosemary, tansy, St John's wort, various mints, and clove pinks. They also grew native herbs introduced to them by North American Indians. These eventually found their way back to Europe, and included American mandrake, blackroot and Jo Pye weed (now a hardy herbaceous perennial, *Eupatorium purpureum*, in many European gardens). Herbs for dyeing were also very important in the traditional American herb garden, and included alkanet, whose root yields a maroon-red dye; weld and marigold, both of which produce a yellow dye; bloodroot which provides an orange dye; sorrel for a yellowish-green colour; and woad and indigo, which were invaluable for dyeing clothes blue.

In the early twentieth century new designs based on the medieval compartmentalizing principle were introduced by such garden designers as Gertrude Jekyll, and included cartwheel or clock patterns, where triangular beds radiate like slices of sponge cake from a central point, and ladders or spirals. Such layouts also lend themselves well to producing herbs in a restricted spot. Jekyll also approved of growing herbs in pots, a practice stretching back to Roman times when city dwellers grew many of their herbs (and other plants too) in containers made of terracotta, and it would have been a common sight to see container herbs on balconies and windowsills. Herbs suitable for containers include basil, rosemary, parsley, marjoram, sage and chives.

Pests and diseases There are a few herbs that can be usefully grown to help prevent pests and diseases in the garden, the most effective being wormwood, southernwood, tansy, rosemary, woodruff, mugwort and lavender.

The bitter aromatic herb wormwood (*Artemisia absinthium*) is said to be effective indoors and out against fleas and many other insects,

Early twentieth-century herb gardens made extensive use of such surfaces as bricks or paving and were often inspired by formal Italian garden designs.

Annual herbs such as this borage will self-seed prolifically in almost every kind of growing conditions. All that is needed is a parent plant or a first packet of seeds – nature will do the rest.

including flies and moths, and an infusion can be made to use as a spray. Southernwood, which is a relative of wormwood, is also said to be an effective deterrent against most insects, notably moths and butterflies. Traditionally, moths have also been kept at bay by lavender, rosemary and woodruff. These would have been dried and the flowers or sprigs placed among clothes and linen, often in muslin bags. In former times bunches of tansy were hung near meat to keep flies away. Another interesting herb is horsetail, which contains cobalt, calcium and silica, and which was used as a fungicide for mildew and blackspot on roses.

Saladings If there is space, it should not be difficult to extend the herbery to include a small production of saladings or limited quantities of vegetables. There are varieties of lettuce these days, such as 'Lollo Rosso' or 'Red Sails', which can be harvested a leaf at a time and others, such as 'Little Gem', which grow small. Then there are the older, traditional green salads, such as lamb's lettuce, winter cress, corn salad and burnet, which Mrs Loudon (1846) mentions in passing as 'used in salads, particularly on the Continent, but they are

seldom grown for that purpose in England.' In spite of her dismissive remarks, such plants are excellent providers of spicy foliage for mixed salads which are evidently more popular everywhere now than they were in 1846. Other fine old salad plants enjoying a revival include sorrel, which is used in soup and salad; radishes, both winter and summer; and land cress. One delicious vegetable, the courgette or zucchini squash, would have been far too invasive and sprawling for a restricted space for Mrs Loudon's day, but happily comes, nowadays, in a compact or bush form, enabling it to be grown in a much smaller space. A single plant will provide a weekly feed for four people at the height of the growing season, and occupies a space no more than 90 sq cm (3 sq ft) in the garden.

As well as being laid out as a self-contained feature, a herb garden, miniaturized or not, would also be suitable for incorporating into a larger kitchen garden. Alternatively, herbs and some salad crops can be used to decorate the edges of food-growing beds, or could furnish the ground at the feet of espalier or cordon fruit trees. Small, decorative thymes are especially useful in this respect, and can be planted alternately with flowering plants such as pansies and sweet violets or with other herbs such as chives. Remember, though, that caution is needed with invasive herbs. Plants with creeping rootstocks such as mint or tansy must be carefully sited and preferably contained so that they do not become pests.

> ❝ *G*OOD HUSWIVES PROVIDE, ERE AN SICKNESS DO COME, OF SUNDRY GOOD THINGS IN HER HOUSE TO HAVE SOME. ❞
>
> Thomas Tusser, 1557

ROTATIONAL CROPPING

An early farming community to use crop rotation was the Amish, who founded their sect in Switzerland in the seventeenth century. They later moved to North America, where to this day they have continued to be renowned for their self-sufficiency and excellent horticultural skills. The scientific basis for rotation in agriculture was observed by Lord Coke of Norfolk, England.

Crop rotation is something that the amateur kitchen gardener with a small plot is tempted to overlook, but rotation is a worthy discipline, contributing to a healthy, well-balanced soil, plant vigour and reducing the occurrence of pests and diseases.

Rotation entails growing closely related vegetable crops in a new plot each year. By rotating crops, the risk of diseases carrying over is reduced. The soil is also given the chance to replenish itself and, by growing vegetable families together, the soil can also be treated to suit their particular needs; for example, some vegetables, such as cabbages, prefer a well-manured ground, others, like carrots and beets, thrive in poorer soil. Rotation is definitely not a cure-all, but has long been recognized as good stewardship of the land.

The three main groups of vegetables are onions, leeks, salad crops, beans and peas; then potatoes and root vegetables such as parsnips, carrots and beetroot; and finally the cabbage family, which includes cabbages, turnips, swedes and Brussels sprouts. A simple rotation plan would be to divide a garden into three plots, one for each family of vegetables. Each year a vegetable group is then moved one plot along, and the soil treated according to the needs of its new occupants. Other traditional gardeners swear by a four-plot plan, which means that each year one plot is left fallow or planted with a nitrogen-enriching crop such as clover, but most gardeners with a small kitchen garden will find the three-plot plan perfectly adequate and easy to manage.

GROWING FRUIT

Fruit, especially top fruit, is hungrier for space than are herbs or vegetables, yielding less in weight per square metre (square yard) but making up for this in the value of the crop. In an old orchard, especially one planted in the first half of this century or earlier, apple trees might spread to 6 m (20 ft) or more across, aged pears commonly grew to 9 m (30 ft) or more in height, and some mature cherries could grow even higher and wider.

Happily, because almost all such fruit varieties are grafted, it is still possible to grow most of the old varieties but on trees of a much more practicable size. The secret lies in the root stock. Modern stocks have been developed at horticultural research institutions that, even when budded with the old varieties, result in plants of a much more manageable size. Different stocks have been raised to suit different growing areas, so cataloguing them here might be misleading, but any local fruit expert will be able to advise on which stock is best suited to your particular soil and climate. Even more specialist stocks also make it possible to grow certain apples, pears and plums in cordons, in small espaliers or even as 'step-over' trees trained to mark the edge of a border by

Apple blossom is among the loveliest of spring flowers. To ensure successful cross-pollination for a good crop, several compatible varieties of apple are needed. Different varieties which flower at the same time will tend to improve pollination but a floriferous crab apple such as Malus *x* hillieri *is even better.*

> 66 *For* THE MAIN GARDEN, I DO NOT DENY BUT THERE SHOULD BE SOME FAIR ALLEYS RANGED ON BOTH SIDES, WITH FRUIT-TREES, AND SOME PRETTY TUFTS OF FRUIT TREES AND ARBOURS WITH SEATS, SET IN SOME DECENT ORDER. 99
>
> Francis Bacon, 1625

growing a pair of horizontal branches as near as 30 cm (12 in) from the ground.

With the revival of interest in old fruit varieties, and with the current trend to conserve them, the choice is growing all the time. Several institutions have been set up with the specific aim of keeping many of the less popular old breeds alive in special orchards and plantations, but there is much that amateur gardeners can do to conserve old varieties too: simply grow them and enjoy them! Clearly, there is no especial virtue in growing the 'has-beens', such as 'Slap-my-girdle' apples and 'Yellow egg' plums, of the apple, pear or plum world unless they have a lot to offer, and it would be unwise to exclude modern varieties simply because they are not old, but so many of the names from the past conjure up especially mouthwatering memories. For apples there are 'Allington Pippin', 'Worcester Pearmain', 'Granny Smiths', and 'Winter Banana'. Some of the classic pears include 'Autumn Bergamot', 'Doyenné du Comice', and 'Williams Red'. Amongst the plums we find 'Old Green Gage', 'Warwickshire Drooper', and 'Prune Damson'.

These varieties are still relatively popular and there are hundreds more, of course, many of them growing in publicly funded orchards which are being preserved as fruit collections. Such institutions also grow varieties which are of historical or horticultural interest only, but it is satisfying to know that they *are* being preserved, if for no other reason than that they carry unique combinations of genes – heritable characteristics – that might become valuable to future generations when tastes have changed or when new diseases come to haunt our commercial orchards.

Then there are ancient kinds of fruit which have, to a great extent, dropped out of favour. The Cornelian cherry (*Cornus mas*) beloved of the Romans would probably be considered too capricious in its cropping and its bearing of fruit too small and fiddly to bother with, but medlars, which had to be rotted or 'bletted' before they were fit to eat, are said to be delicious. The fruit of the service tree (*Sorbus domestica*) was once eaten, apparently, and I can vouch personally for the quince – a beautiful plant whose fruit, when cooked, has the most distinctive flavour of any I have tasted. Blended with apple, its sharp, citrus-like tang can turn an autumn pie into a special occasion.

Besides trees, soft fruits such as gooseberries, loganberries or, as here, redcurrants, will ripen sooner grown against a warm wall than if they are left free-standing. They also provide a decorative cover.

'Conference' is an old European breed of pear with elongated greenish fruits, sweet flavour and superb keeping qualities. It is one of the best varieties for a small orchard.

SHAPING FRUIT TREES

Training fruit trees into shapes against some form of support, such as a wall, is an example of period gardening that adapts well to the modern garden, particularly where space is confined. In medieval times, fruit arches were popular in monasteries, and it would be possible to reconstruct one today using a tunnel framework (these can be bought in kit form or you can make your own out of wood) and growing the trees as cordons (see opposite). Later, trees were trained against walls to take advantage of the heat stored in them, thus minimizing frost damage and forcing fruit to ripen early. They were also used by early gardeners to form barriers between different areas of the garden, thus saving space.

Gardeners in Europe soon discovered that a sunny south wall was ideal for growing figs, peaches and nectarines, while apples, plums, gages and pears could be grown against east or west walls. For fixing trees to the wall Stephen Switzer recommended in *The Practical Fruit-Gardener* (1752) 'little Wooden Peggs, made of the Heart of Oak, drove into the Wall between the Bricks, to which may be ty'd all the Small Branches with Juncus or small Rush . . . and all the great Boughs requiring more Strength, may with small Withies, made of Oziers or Basket Rods, be ty'd to large wooden Peggs . . . ' The advantage of this method, Switzer pointed out, is that 'as soon as the Fruit Boughs swell out to the Extent of the Rush or Withy, that band will easily give Way, and not pinch or damage the Tree, and the Peggs of Wood also being round, will not gall or fret the young Branches.' Nowadays we have vine-eyes instead of wooden pegs, which are designed to be driven into the mortar. The wire is then threaded through the 'eyes'. The branches should be protected as Switzer recommends, placing bamboo canes where the tree is to be trained and tying it with soft string – anything stiffer will chafe the bark.

The same applies when using a support made out of wire and posts. As a general rule, the wire should be strung between stout posts or against an existing fence or wall at 60 cm (2 ft) intervals or, for espaliers, the width you want the branches to be apart.

Ideal wall plants for the kitchen garden include this blackberry, whose ferny foliage makes a fresh green cove and whose sharp, tangy fruits are perfect for such old-fashioned recipes as blackberry and apple crumble.

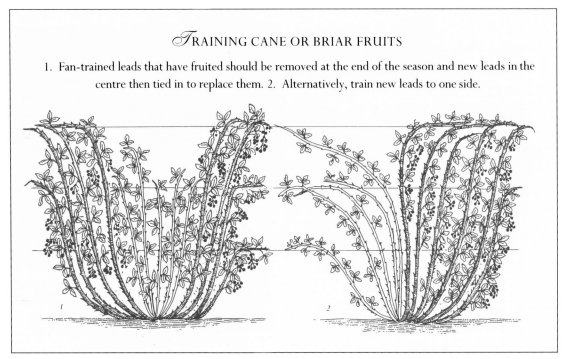

TRAINING CANE OR BRIAR FRUITS

1. Fan-trained leads that have fruited should be removed at the end of the season and new leads in the centre then tied in to replace them. 2. Alternatively, train new leads to one side.

𝒯RAINING A CORDON

1. Prune young trees to acquire the cordon shape. 2. Begin to create fruiting spurs by cutting back.
3. Restrict branching to retain cordon shape. 4. Remove young growths to three buds (to about 7.5–12 cm/3–5 in) each summer and re-tie to avoid wind damage.

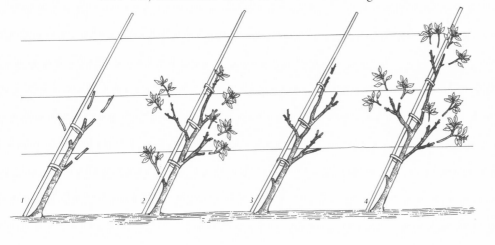

When pruning shoots, make sure that there is a little space between stem and bud, as on the right; the cut on the left is too close to the bud. Always cut above a bud that will grow outwards.

𝑀ULTIPLE CORDON

To increase fruiting potential from each tree, two or even three main stems can be allowed to develop. The pruning technique, once the stems have grown, is exactly as for cordons or espaliers.

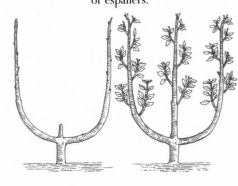

Cordons These are the easiest for the amateur to achieve. A cordon is made up of a series of single fruit stems spaced about 75 cm (2½ ft) apart, each one grown at an angle of about 45 degrees to the ground. They are often trained free-standing to form a barrier, using wire supports strung between posts, although the cordon design can also be used against walls and fences. They should be allowed to grow to a maximum height of 1.8 m (6 ft).

In late summer, wall fruits can be tied in to prevent damage from autumn winds. Pruning of members of the plum family should, however, be kept to a minimum to avoid infection from silver leaf disease.

The French were masters at training fruit trees. From the 1700s onwards, they excelled in creating fabulous shapes to resemble coronets, vases, even goblets, and the fashion for such bizarre creations spread far and wide. Fortunately, there are also four basic forms that have served gardeners well over the centuries: cordons, fans, espaliers and step-overs.

These old espalier trees have been pruned regularly year by year until their branches bristle with stubby fruiting spurs.

maximum height of 2.5 m (8 ft).

Espaliers Here, the branches are trained in a series of horizontal tiers between 30 cm (12 in) and 60 cm (2 ft) apart. They should be planted between 3.6 m (12 ft) and 4.5 m (15 ft) apart, and allowed to grow to a maximum height of 2.5 m (8 ft).

Step-overs As the name implies, these are fruit trees whose branches have been trained in a single tier set low enough to be stepped over. It is a technique that is best suited to apples and pears. The usual height for a step-over is about 23 cm (9 in), and each tree should be planted a minimum of 3 m (10 ft) apart up to 4.5 m (15 ft).

Fans This is a good shape for cherries, plums, nectarines and peaches. Fans are most often seen grown against walls, but, like cordons, they can also be grown using a support consisting of wires and posts. A fan is usually created by allowing several stems to grow straight from the main stem at acute angles. Depending on the fruit, trees should be planted between 3 m (10 ft) and 3.6 m (12 ft) apart, and grown to a

The kitchen garden can be purely functional, but in many modern situations it is preferable to mix food with ornament. Even if you do not wish to raise much in the way of food, or, if you prefer to concentrate on flowers and foliage in your garden, there are still planting opportunities for raising a little of your own food. Training a fruit tree on a wall will give many years of crops and look lovely too,

ℐRAINING A FAN

The main branches should be pruned back to the original shape each summer. Canes can be used in addition to strengthen young branches.

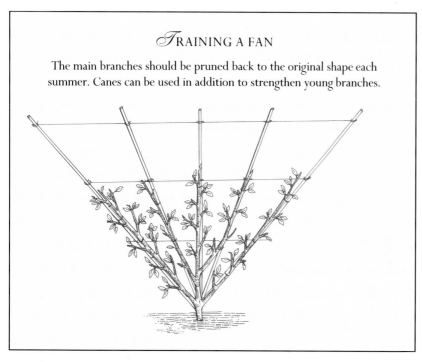

𝒜RCURE

A fruit tree is trained to form a series of horizontal arches.

whether early in the year, when its blossom might be the crowning glory of the spring display, or later, when the fruit looks so colourful you can hardly bear to pick it.

In a mixed border, a small fruit tree planted as a focal point can make the perfect combination of beauty and function. Among flowers, it is also possible not only to grow a wide range of herbs but also to plant small groups of vegetables which can be harvested, albeit in modest amounts, without ruining, and indeed often enhancing, your planting schemes.

A good all-round apple, 'Charles Ross' is sweet enough to eat fresh yet sharp enough to make a delicious apple pie.

TRAINING A STEP-OVER OR ESPALIER

1. At planting in winter, remove all but the four most favourably positioned branches. 2. Tie these into position on training wires or with canes. 3. Thereafter, prune side-shoots every summer like a cordon.

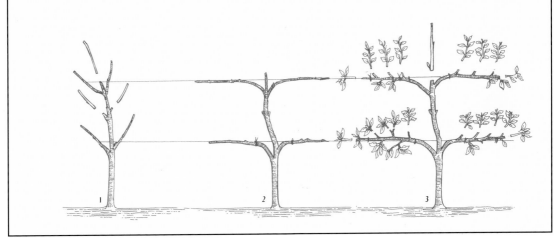

TRAINING A FESTOON

Extra fruiting is stimulated by straining the limbs downward. 1. Tie the main lead down at the end of the first summer. 2. Each summer remove small shoots as for cordons. 3. Tie down secondary limbs as they develop. 4. After several seasons, remove ties; the branches will remain bent.

Old-fashioned plants

The 'Victoria' plum is one of the finest of the old-fashioned breeds with its rosy skin, golden flesh and subtle flavour.

The changes that have been achieved, over the last millenium, with such staple crops as carrots, tomatoes and the cabbage tribe, are so profound that the modern plants have little in common with their wild forebears. There are notable exceptions, such as raspberries or some of the leafy herbs, which are similar to the species from which they originate, but almost everything we grow for food now is the result of a long legacy of development and improvement.

Over the last few decades, the plant breeders' motivation has moved away from such desirable aspects as flavour to the more commercial considerations of appearance, size, yield and shelf-life. Modern varieties of strawberries, for instance, are large, look delicious and stay wholesome on the supermarket shelf for much longer than old varieties, but they are almost completely tasteless!

Sadly, many of the old cultivars have disappeared. With European legislation curtailing seed lists and international restrictions on seed traffic, old breeds are dropping out every year. In many countries, however, there are specialist conservation societies with seed exchanges and a small range of 'antique' plants can still be obtained from the modern horticultural industry. A limited selection of fruit and vegetable botanical families are described in this chapter which have been included either because they are useful croppers in the kitchen garden, or because they contain notable older varieties or species that are still available but which have, undeservedly, gone out of fashion.

Unlike ornamental plants, where needs vary hugely, most vegetable crops have the same requirements – namely, deeply worked, fertile soil, plenty of daylight and as much shelter from cold winds as possible. Leafy crops such as spinach and brassicas are hungry for nitrogen, whereas root crops and fruits – carrots and tomatoes – usually need additions of phosphorous and potash. In the case of nitrogen, however, excessive levels should be avoided, both in chemical form or from too much fresh manure, as it can make roots grow 'fangy' – that is, subdivide into small roots.

The majority of vegetables are raised from seed each season, with the exception of perennials such as artichokes and asparagus.

In Britain, traditional allotments enabled those without land of their own to grow food. Many plots are now a century old, and allotment holders still continue to grow a wide range of old-fashioned vegetables and fruit.

Early breeds of lettuce were
more bitter and less densely
leafed than modern forms
like these, and were probably
no more disease-resistant.
The new varieties are,
however, perfectly in keeping
with old-fashioned gardening
methods.

CHENOPODIACEAE

The beet family: beetroot, spinach, Swiss chard, good King Henry

'The root of garden or red beet is exceedingly wholesome and nutritious.' Mrs Beeton, *The Book of Household Management*, 1861

Wholesome in root and leaf, a useful source of mineral salts and delicious in all kinds of cuisine, the beet family has a long tradition in the kitchen garden and contributes much to the healthy diet. Most beets prefer a light, sandy soil which has been well manured the previous year.

For use in a traditional French-style potager, the colourful stems of Swiss chard add ornament to utility. Both red and white stemmed varieties can be sown in spring or late summer to make a colourful display and to provide succulent leaf stalks and slightly bitter though nourishing foliage over a long period.

COMPOSITAE

The daisy family: artichokes, cardoons, lettuce, endive, scorzonera, skirret

'The flower "heads" must be of an even size, not coarse or irregular, with a smooth, clear skin.' The *Gardeners' Inquire Within*, on globe artichokes

This is an important family for salad crops. Modern lettuces are in fact more succulent, sweet, and crisp than older cultivars, so there is little advantage in growing any of the old varieties in preference to current ones. Endive, on the other hand, has been less extensively developed and is delicious in its earlier forms. It was a firm favourite with nineteenth-century gardeners, as were cardoons – thistle-like plants whose young shoots had to be blanched before harvesting – and both globe and Jerusalem artichokes, which are perennials and can be cropped for several years.

Root crops in the daisy family were popular

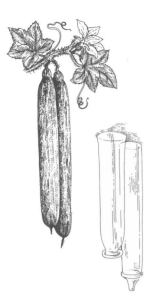

Cucumbers and nineteenth-century cucumber straightening glasses.

until superseded by heavier-yielding plants. Skirret, with its small, knobbly tubers, is really of botanical interest only nowadays, but scorzonera and salsify, both of which have slender, tapering roots, are delicious vegetables, easy to grow and will tolerate soil of only moderate fertility.

CRUCIFERAE

The cabbage family: brassicas, turnips, seakale, swedes, radishes, rape, cress

'Training is everything . . . cauliflower is nothing but cabbage with a college education.' Mark Twain, *Pudd'nhead Wilson*, 1894

One of the oldest of the vegetable families, coleworts were prized for their leaves in medieval times and have since developed into a whole range of root or leafy vegetables. They

By providing warmth and darkness in the middle of winter, this seakale plant has been enticed to throw up a forest of succulent young shoots.

are hungry crops, growing best in well dunged ground. Seakale was a popular delicacy in the nineteenth century, but is less common nowadays and would be worth reviving in the kitchen garden. As it grows naturally on sea coasts, this perennial will thrive in a sandy loam and must be forced to produce crisp white stalks (see page 25) in autumn and winter.

CUCURBITACEAE

The cucumber family: cucumbers, melons, marrows, squashes, gherkins

'By the Eastern nations generally as well as by the Greeks and Romans, it was greatly esteemed.' Mrs Beeton, on cucumbers, 1861

The cucurbitaceae family consists mainly of climbing plants, all which have been grown for many centuries. Most of them are tender annuals and so need starting off under glass in colder climates, either on hotbeds or with artificial heating. Later, they need constant feeding to crop well and prefer a damp ground. Glasshouse cucumbers were favourites of the nineteenth-century gentry, whose gardeners grew them in special glass sheaths to keep them straight and tender. Greenhouse cucumbers are female and must be unfertilized to prevent a bitter flavour in the fruits.

For sheer bulk, the traditional pumpkins grown in North America must be one of the heaviest yielders. These were valuable food crops for early settlers, because they could be stored through the long cold winters (see page 48), and not surprisingly many more interesting pumpkins and squashes have been developed in North America than in Europe. Melons can be grown in cold, northern climates, but ripen best in sub-tropical conditions at Mediterranean latitudes. All respond well to a fast, warm-growing season and to heavy feeds of organic manures.

Courgettes, or zucchini squashes, are usually harvested in their infancy, but they will mature to fine marrows with long-keeping qualities.

ℒILIACEAE

The lily family: asparagus, leeks, shallots, garlic, onions

'All onions are sharpe and move teares by the smell.'
John Gerard, *Herball*, 1633

Onions, shallots and garlic pre-date Roman times, not only as flavouring herbs, but also as valuable medicinal substances. The decongesting property of garlic, for example, was recog-nized by medieval physicians and pills made from garlic oil are still widely used today.

Asparagus is a perennial plant and needs more patience, but it is one of the most succulent and distinctly flavoured vegetables in the kitchen garden. Mrs Loudon (1846) recommends its culture in deeply worked raised beds – a system that has yet to be bettered – and such old varieties as 'Connovers Colossal' are still used in many gardens.

ℐOLANACEAE

The tomato family: potatoes, tomatoes, peppers, chillis, aubergines, cape gooseberries
'There is a foolish notion abroad, that certain Potatoes have deteriorated in quality . . . Those who hold this doctrine can know very little of practice.' Annals of Horticulture, 1846

For more than four hundred years since their introduction, potatoes have been a valuable source of starchy food all over Europe and, later, in North America. Their breeding has developed more rapidly than ever in recent decades, but not for the best. Older varieties, except those that have become too disease-prone to grow, tend to be superior in flavour and character and are therefore of greater interest to the private gardener than those bred purely for heavy yield. 'Pink Fir Apple' for example and the French 'Rattee' are forms of the old 'Continental Yellow', or 'German Fingl-ing', both of which have a delicious flavour and waxy texture.

Tomatoes, mentioned in Gerard and grown in Europe since the beginning of the Renais-sance, have also suffered from modern breed-ing, but happily there has been a consumer backlash. New, small-fruited varieties such as 'Gardener's Delight' seem to carry something of the old-fashioned sweet flavour and are becoming widely available.

UMBELLIFERAE

The carrot family: carrots, celery, parsnips

'*. . . sowe Carrets in your Gardens, and humbly praise God for them, as for a singular and great blessing . . .*'
Richard Gardiner, 1597

Plants in this family are often known as 'kecks' or, in Shakespeare, 'kecksies' – possibly referring to their hollow stems. (Trousers in parts of northern England are known colloquially as 'keks'.) Their flowers are mostly white or yellow, and, though tiny, are beautifully arranged in umbels on the stems. Ornamental umbellifers include 'Queen Anne's Lace' and the lovely astrantias, but it is as food crops that this family excels.

For sheer bulk, in poor soil and an unforgiving climate, carrots and parsnips are among the most productive of vegetables. In the restricted space of a medieval monastery garden, such bounteous croppers were much valued, and in modern gardens where space is restricted, these are good vegetables to select. Carrots can be sown in succession for continuity, but parsnips are usually drilled in spring for a single autumn crop.

Celery is more difficult to grow, demanding rich, deeply manured soil and warm growing conditions. Celeriac can be greedy for space, but both its root, which makes a delicious nutty-flavoured purée, and its leaves, which can be used for flavouring, are edible.

Herbs

Most gardeners are spoilt for choice when it comes to selecting herbs for the garden since there are so many excellent species to choose from; some, however, have become kitchen and garden classics, and will appear at the top of most people's list of plants to include in a border, as a useful hedging plant to border paths, or as part of a formal herb garden.

CORIANDRUM SATIVUM

Coriander, dizzycorn, cilantro

'*Its young leaves are put into soups and salads, and the seeds are extensively employed in confectionary, for disguising the taste of medicines, and by distillers . . .*'
The Gardener's Assistant, 1859

Young coriander leaves add a delicious, spicy note to salads and soups, while the dried seeds, with their sweet, warm aroma, are a well-known ingredient in spice and curry mixtures. Gerard (1633) recommended an infusion of coriander seeds as an aid for digestion, and they have been used for centuries as a flavouring; the seeds are delicious crushed and rubbed into lamb and other meats, for example, and they are also good added whole or crushed to pastries and cakes.

Coriander is an attractive half-hardy annual (H 45 cm/18 in) with very pale pink flowers in summer. It requires a light, well-drained soil in full sun, and can be increased by seed sown in spring after the last frost.

LAVANDULA ANGUSTIFOLIA

Lavender

'*Lavender is almost wholly spent with us, for to perfume linnen, apparrell, gloves, leather, & the dryed flowers to comfort and dry up the moisture of a cold braine.*' John Parkinson, *Paradisi in Sole, Paradisus Terrestris*, 1629

The Greeks and Romans liked to add lavender flowers to their water when bathing, and it is not surprising therefore that its name comes from the Latin *lavare*, to wash. Later, in medieval times, lavender became an important strewing herb, and it was also placed among household linen and clothes to keep them sweet-smelling and free of moths. Lavender continues to be much in demand these days as a major ingredient of toilet waters, and as a

Thinning carrots

Coriander

Basil

Right: the plantswoman Gertrude Jekyll was fond of lavender and used it in much of her planting, allowing it, as here at Hestercombe in England, to spill over and soften the harsh lines of paving.

Left: old-fashioned lavender growers would cut the stems for drying just as the blooms opened to guarantee maximum fragrance. Gentle drying ensures good colour preservation.

fragrance in a wide range of toiletries (as an essential oil, it is also used a great deal in aromatherapy, where its calming, sedative properties are highly rated).

In the garden, lavender is a very useful hardy evergreen perennial, and its bushy form (H 75–90 cm/2½–3 ft) is often used as an edging for paths. Lavender will thrive in quite poor, light soil, but it does need a sunny position in the garden. It can be increased by cuttings taken in autumn, or it can be grown from seed.

OCIMUM BASILICUM
Basil, sweet basil

'The smell of Basil is good for the heart . . . it taketh away sorrowfulness, which commeth of melancholy and maketh a man merry and glad.' John Gerard, 1633

Basil is a marvellous culinary herb, and there is nothing quite like the fresh leaves chopped up and added to a tomato salad or a classic Italian pesto sauce. It was known of in Egyptian times, and it was a very popular herb with the Greeks and Romans, who valued its antiseptic and soothing qualities.

Basil is a low-growing tender annual (H 20–45 cm/8–18 in) and as such it is a useful pot herb (the Romans probably grew it as a container herb). It needs full sun in a well-sheltered position, and the soil should be rich, well-drained but moist. Basil can be grown from seed in late spring.

ORIGANUM VULGARE
Wild marjoram, oregano

'The whole plant is of a sweet smell and sharp biting taste.' John Gerard, 1633

The red-stemmed oregano is a native bush of the Mediterranean, where it grows very freely, and the Romans are known to have used it widely as a culinary and medicinal herb; today, it's still a popular herb for the kitchen in Italy and Greece, and its distinctive flavour is to be found in many traditional Italian pizza and spaghetti dishes.

Oregano is a hardy perennial (H 15–30 cm/6–12 in) and produces purple or pink flowers in summer; it will grow in quite poor, light soil, although it needs a sunny position at the front of the border to grow well. It can be propagated by cuttings taken early in the summer, by division of roots in spring or autumn, or by seed in spring.

The other varieties of marjoram traditionally grown in the garden are the half-hardy *O. majorana* (H 20 cm/8 in), the mauve-flowered sweet marjoram, which is used to flavour meat, fish and cheese dishes; and *O. onites* (H to 60 cm/2 ft), pot marjoram, which has pink and white flowers in summer.

ℛ OSMARINUS OFFICINALIS
Rosemary
'Here's rosemary, that's for remembrance.'
Shakespeare, *Hamlet*

This hardy evergreen shrub originates from the Mediterranean, where it has been valued for thousands of years as a culinary and medicinal herb. As an aromatic pot herb, its pungent flavour complements a wide range of pork, lamb and fish dishes, and it is equally good in sweet biscuits, syrups and jams, although a little will go a long way! Rosemary is believed to be a tonic for the brain and is said to improve the memory – hence Ophelia's line from *Hamlet* – but it is perhaps most famous as one of the key ingredients in Eau-de-Cologne; it was also the principal herb in Hungary water, which the Queen of Hungary used as a rejuvenating lotion for her face.

Rosemary, which bears delicate, pale blue flowers in summer, will grow well in any light garden soil in a sheltered, sunny position, but it is well to know that some varieties can grow very high (H up to 2 m/6½ ft). It can be increased by cuttings taken in late summer, or from seed in late summer.

𝒯 HYMUS VULGARIS
Garden thyme
'. . . it helpeth the Lethargie, frensie and madnesse . . .' John Gerard, 1633

Many thymes have a creeping habit (in ancient times they were used for lawns), but garden thyme, which is the most popular variety for culinary purposes, grows more in a low hummock (H 30 cm/12 in) with very pale mauve to pink flowers in summer. It is a delicious herb in many meat dishes, particularly in slow-cooking stews and casseroles to which wine has been

Rosemary

Culinary thyme is a bushy plant with small, lilac-coloured flowers but the species that Shakespeare's Oberon refers to – 'I know a bank where the wild thyme grows' – is Thymus serpyllum. *This comes in quite a range of glowing colours from deep purple through pink to pure white.*

Thyme

The fruits of many old English varieties, like this 'St Edmund', have a roughened texture known as 'russet'. Most russet varieties have outstanding keeping qualities.

Right: in an old well-established apple orchard, the trees may be growing out of turf, perhaps with wild flowers among the grasses and spring bulbs, such as daffodils, to provide colour early in the year. Growing young trees in this way is feasible provided the sward is killed off around the tree roots to prevent the grasses from damaging the young trees.

added (it is also a classic ingredient in bouquet garni). A tisane of thyme is said to aid digestion (Gerard particularly recommended it for the 'wambling and gripings of the bellie'), and it has also been used as a cough mixture.

Thyme is an evergreen perennial which will grow in a chalky (limestone or alkaline) soil, in a sheltered, sunny position. It can be increased by division in spring, by sowing seed in spring, or by cuttings in summer.

Fruit

Even in the tiniest kitchen garden there is likely to be room if not for a dwarf or trained fruit tree, then for small bushes or neat cordons of currants and gooseberries. Climbing soft fruit such as loganberries, boysenberries or tayberries can also be used to good effect in an ornamental kitchen garden trained against walls or free-standing.

APPLES AND PEARS

'Plant pears for heirs.' Country saying, illustrating the long interval between planting a pear tree and when it bears fruit.

Tree fruits were in cultivation since Ancient Egypt. Historically, these were long-term crops, requiring grafting and not bearing fruit for several years after planting out. Nowadays, with scientifically developed rooting stock, many of the old varieties can be grown as compact trees. Dwarfing rootstocks enable them to fruit earlier and to be grown in restricted areas; indeed, there are even stocks which enable small fruit trees to spend their whole lives in containers.

Fruit was produced out of season in the eighteenth and nineteenth centuries by forcing containerized stock in a heated orchard house, and this can be effected even more easily nowadays using varieties grafted on to modern

dwarfing stocks. Apples and pears which are forced in this way, in a conservatory perhaps, should be restored to a more 'normal' life as soon as they have fruited.

Among new varieties, mention must be made of Ballerina trees. These are wholly modern in concept and grow as stout single stems, but, because of their distinctive shape, they are of great architectural value in a traditional kitchen garden where space is too limited for extensive cordons or espaliers. To date, there are several dessert varieties, including 'Flamenco' and 'Bolero' and one cooker known as 'Charlotte'. Older varieties of merit include the sweet, nutty-flavoured pippins, such as 'Ribston Pippin', 'Allington Pippin' and 'Cox's Orange Pippin'.

MEDLARS AND QUINCES

'. . . the woman with childe, which eateth many Quinces during the time of her breeding, shall bring forth wise children and of good understanding.' John Gerard, 1633

Beloved of the Elizabethans as a fruit for flavouring all kinds of dishes, both sweet and savoury, the quince is a perfect tree for today's traditional gardener. The fruits are long-lasting, borne on gracefully branching trees whose pale pink and white spring blossom makes an attractive bonus.

Medlars were once prized as delicacies to be 'bletted' or rotted before fit for consumption. As a central tree in the kitchen garden, their shapely habit and pretty blossom in spring

Below: the quince makes a fine ornamental plant, with arching branches and interesting winter bark, and its fruit is excellent for jellies and for adding to fruit pies.

Above: the attractive tan hue of this half-grown 'Doyenné du Comice' fades as the fruit ripens.

make them assets even though modern growers might flinch from the idea of eating the strange-looking fruits.

$\mathscr{P}$EACHES, PLUMS AND THEIR ALLIES

'In August comes plums of all sorts in fruit, pears, apricots, barberries . . . of all colours.' Francis Bacon, *Of Gardens*, 1625

Botanically, these stone fruit are known as 'drupes'. Their queen is undoubtedly the peach, which would have been grown against a sunny wall in old kitchen gardens in the colder regions. For best results, these should be fan-trained (see page 34), maximizing the spread of the branches on the warm surface of the stone or brick; apricots enjoy similar treatment.

Plums range from tiny hedgerow damsons to the huge round monsters bred in the great kitchen gardens of the nineteenth century; among the old varieties, the golden-green bullace and the French 'Reine Claude' are some of the most flavoursome for cooking purposes. For fresh eating, the English plum 'Victoria' has been prized for decades.

$\mathscr{S}$TRAWBERRIES

'Wife unto the garden and set me a plot
With strawberry roots of the best to be got.'
Thomas Tusser, *Five Hundred Points of Good Husbandry*, 1557

Perhaps overrated because the flavour so seldom lives up to expectations, these plump, glistening red fruits are surely among the most luscious grown. Gardeners of the Middle Ages probably grew wood strawberries, whose fruits were smaller, but whose taste was sweeter and more fragrant than modern hybrids.

Work has been done to eradicate the viruses

that debilitated some of the old varieties such as 'Late Pine' and 'Royal Sovereign' and to bring them back as a commercial crop. These may not yield as heavily as modern cultivars but they do have more flavour. For the small ornamental kitchen garden, wood strawberries are another variety worth growing. They are easily raised from seed and make a pretty plant for underplanting free-standing espalier fruit trees. Better still, they will yield continuously throughout the summer.

The older varieties of strawberries may not be so high-yielding and may have less resistance to disease, but they are so much better flavoured than commercial fruits.

Storing and preserving

A glance at any of the old books on kitchen garden management will show that much of the skill of the fruit and vegetable grower lay not in just how much he could produce, but in how he could provide an interesting selection of fresh produce all through the year, and store and preserve as much as possible as effectively as possible. This chapter looks at ways in which the bounty of the old-fashioned garden can be spread throughout the year by using special methods to store and preserve produce.

Storing

In the right conditions, a great many vegetables will store after harvest for months. Carrots, rutabagas, parsnips and potatoes last well in the coolness and darkness of a cellar, especially if they are packed in moist peat or peaty material. Few houses are equipped with generous cellars these days, but most gardeners are able to find somewhere cool but frost-free, such as a garage or garden shed. In North America, the root cellar is a popular old-fashioned system of storing root crops, apples and winter squashes. This consists of a small room, about 3 m by 3 m (10 ft by 10 ft), sunk into the ground and built of brick or stone. Apart from plenty of shelf space, some root cellars also included a water trough for keeping fish alive.

VEGETABLES

Onions and shallots will last a whole winter and part of spring hung up in an airy environment. The secret is to ensure that they are absolutely dry with crispy skins. The stringing process itself is simply a matter of plaiting the dead, but still flexible, foliage and tying the plait with a piece of stout twine. An easy alternative is to store them in clean old stockings or tights with a knot between each onion to prevent them from being in contact with each other. That way, if one or two rot, the others are less likely to be contaminated. However the new 'Sleeper' and 'Keep well' onions developed in North America and Japan resist rotting, even stored on a kitchen shelf at room temperature.

For globe artichokes, *The Gardener's Assistant* (1859) recommends: 'As soon as the crop from each of the flower-stems is gathered they should be cut down; and all dead leaves should be removed at the same time. Any heads remaining in November [autumn] may be preserved for a long time, by cutting them off with the whole of the stalk attached, planting the latter in moist sand in a shed or cellar,

The traditional American root cellar with its steady cool temperature preserved the autumn glut of produce long into winter.

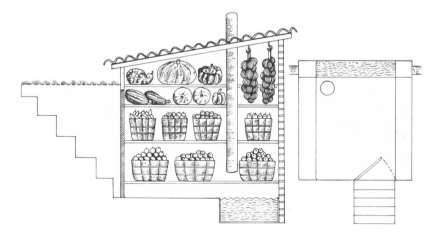

*Above and left: to remain
firm when stored, onions
must be kept completely dry.
Stringing is the traditional
method and works well.*

Pumpkins and gourds must be left in the sun so that their skins will harden, enabling them to be stored indoors later.

Gourds and squashes are useful for decoration and once dry will last indefinitely. Different forms of squashes have distinctive flavours.

secure from frost, and cutting off every three or four days a small portion from the flower part of the stalk.' To keep a globe artichoke for just a few days, place the stem in water.

It was traditional to store members of the marrow tribe – pumpkins, squashes, and so on – harvested in maturity in a cool, frost-free, dry place where they would keep for up to 4 months. Mostly, these are less flavourful than the fresh young fruits of summer, but they do have a place especially when they are creamed or used to make up winter dishes such as pumpkin pie. The spaghetti squash (also called vegetable spaghetti) commonly found in North America is a type of summer squash that produces a hard skin, allowing the large melon-sized fruits to be stored in a cool, dry place for months without spoilage.

Potatoes, parsnips, turnips (in colder climates), carrots, jerusalem artichokes, and beetroots were once regularly stored in a clamp to protect them from the weather. Alfred William

Smith, a market gardener in the nineteenth century, recommended making a clamp in a high but sheltered place where the ground is well drained. The soil was dug out to a depth of 30 cm (12 in) over an area about 1.5 m (5 ft) in diameter. This pit was filled with a thick layer of straw or twigs and the vegetables arranged in a ridge-shaped heap on top to a height of 90–120 cm (3–4 ft). Another layer of straw was placed over the vegetables, at least 30 cm (12 in) thick, followed by a layer at least 23 cm (9 in) of the soil taken out. Funnels of straw were made in the sides or at the top of the clamp for ventilation.

Carrots were piled up to form a cone shape, the top ends of the carrots always facing outwards, and covered in sand only, not straw or soil. The cone shape can also be used for potatoes, although *The Gardener's Assistant* points out that: 'The form of a ridge is more convenient than that of a cone, because, when portions are taken out for use, the breach in the end of the ridge can be more easily closed than one in the side of a conical heap. The ridges should run in the direction north and south, so that if it be necessary to open them in frosty weather, they may be done at the south end, when the sun's rays at noon will prevent that part from being frozen.'

An alternative to the clamp was simply to store root vegetables in boxes filled with sand or sandy soil; in modern times, moist peat or vermiculite is recommended.

Harvested cabbages can be left to hang in a dry, airy place such as an outside shed for one to two weeks, as long as the whole plant is pulled up. Cauliflowers can be stored in the same way for the same length of time, but they should be sprayed regularly with water to keep them fresh. Some nineteenth-century gardeners preferred to bury heads in dry earth in boxes, leaving a portion of the root sticking out above the mound of earth to lay hold of in pulling up the plant.

Some vegetables, of course, are hardy and can be left in the ground and lifted as required, such as jerusalem artichokes, celeriac (but not in cold climates), leeks and swedes.

Left in the ground until required for the pot, winter leeks will stay tender until they begin to bolt in the spring.

Root vegetables preserved in a clamp will stay fresh regardless of the weather conditions outside.

HERBS

The traditional way to preserve herbs for the winter months was to dry them. Mrs Beeton, in *The Book of Household Management* (1861), recommends that herbs should be gathered 'on a very dry day, . . . just before they begin to flower. If this is done when the weather is damp, the herbs will not be so good a colour . . . . They should be perfectly freed from dirt and dust, and be divided into small bunches, with their roots cut off.' Harvested herbs should be dried immediately in a dark, warm place – Mrs Beeton suggested a very hot oven, which would have instantly dried out *all* the flavour and colour from the herbs, but a very low oven would do at a pinch. Better still is an airing cupboard – the important thing is to supply a steady, low heat and ventilation, so keep the airing cupboard or oven door slightly ajar when the herbs are drying. If you are only drying a small amount of herbs, then they can

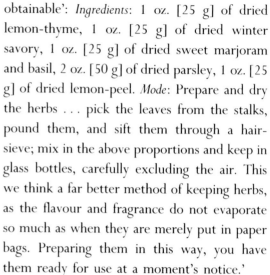

obtainable': *Ingredients*: 1 oz. [25 g] of dried lemon-thyme, 1 oz. [25 g] of dried winter savory, 1 oz. [25 g] of dried sweet marjoram and basil, 2 oz. [50 g] of dried parsley, 1 oz. [25 g] of dried lemon-peel. *Mode*: Prepare and dry the herbs . . . pick the leaves from the stalks, pound them, and sift them through a hair-sieve; mix in the above proportions and keep in glass bottles, carefully excluding the air. This we think a far better method of keeping herbs, as the flavour and fragrance do not evaporate so much as when they are merely put in paper bags. Preparing them in this way, you have them ready for use at a moment's notice.'

Parsley can be stored quite differently, as the following recipe from Mrs Beeton describes: 'Use freshly-gathered parsley for keeping, and wash it perfectly free from grit and dirt; put it into boiling water which has been slightly salted and well skimmed, and then let it boil for 2 or 3 minutes; take it out, let it drain, and lay it on a sieve in front of the fire, when it should be dried as expeditiously as possible. Store it away in a very dry place in bottles, and when wanted for use, pour over it a little warm water, and let it stand for about 5 minutes.'

be spread out on one or two wire racks and placed in the airing cupboard or oven. For the first few days, turn the herbs over regularly and then leave them until they become very brittle but still slightly green – they must not be allowed to go brown. If you are drying larger quantities, then you may need to use large wooden frames and stretch muslin or fine netting over to create larger trays.

When the herbs were dried, in Mrs Beeton's day they would have tied the bunches up and put them in paper bags and kept them in a dry place: a basically sound method as dried herbs deteriorate more rapidly in the light, and need to be kept away from moisture. They last better, however, stored in glass jars in a dark, dry place, in which case the leaves should be removed from the stalks and crushed first. Mrs Beeton herself preferred the following method for keeping herbs 'When fresh herbs are not

Fruit

Apples Certain apples will keep for a surprisingly long period in cool, dry conditions. Middle and late croppers such as 'Cox's Orange Pippin' and 'Blenheim Orange' tend to keep better than the earlier varieties, which are nicest to eat straight off the tree. (Apples are ready to pick when the stalk parts easily from its connection with the spur.) Most of the old russet varieties – apples whose skin is covered with a roughened texture – preserve especially well and have a sweet, nutty flavour, even when they have just begun to wizen. Dorothy Hartley, in *Food in England* (1979), describes how the Norfolk Biffin was dried very slowly in the

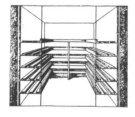

Fruit-room, 1859

bread oven and 'packed down flat in layers as they dried – so that they were red, round, wrinkled "biffins". If the skin burst, they were spoilt, as it was the slowly cooked juice converted within the apple which gave the biffin the advantage over modern apple "rings".' The best long-storage apple of all – the 'Granny Smith' – is an old variety that originated in Australia. Though the original 'Granny Smith' needs a relatively warm, frost-free growing season of at least 150 days, new earlier-maturing strains have been developed.

To protect almost ripe fruit on the trees Stephen Switzer recommended in *The Practical Fruit-Gardener* (1752) tying small bags around individual fruit: 'the cheapest method is the dipping of whited-brown paper bags in Sweet Oil, and putting the bunches when dry therein, and this will preserve them a great while, even till Christmas in a mild time, and will keep the wet from them a great while.' A modern equivalent would simply be brown paper bags.

Old-fashioned harvesting and storing techniques are, in many respects, no different from

Wrapping Fruit

Choose only unblemished apples or pears, wrap individually in dry paper and keep cool but frost-free for the winter.

modern methods and are not difficult to carry out. However, a certain amount of conscientiousness is essential, particularly when deciding which fruits to eat first, and a sharp eye for any faults will also help to ensure success. Many of the old gardening writers recommend picking fruit on a clear, dry day and carefully placing them in baskets lined with straw. When harvesting, windfalls must be gathered and eaten first, and within a few days of their coming off the trees. One blessing of the deep freeze is that if there is a surplus of windfalls, these can be peeled, cored, lightly stewed and then packed and frozen, in which state they will last far longer than they would have done left whole. (An interesting old-fashioned alternative dating back to Anglo Saxon times might be to invest in a small cider press!)

The sight of apples, ripening in the late summer sunshine in the kitchen garden, will inspire even the most faint-hearted of gardeners. Old varieties of fruits such as 'Allington Pippin' or 'Worcester Pearmain' are particularly colourful compared to some of the modern breeds.

The well-deserved fruits of labour: freshly harvested apples from the cottage orchard, homemade chutney and bread and a round of locally produced cheese.

Fruit handbarrow

Market-garden barrow

Any fruit with blemishes should be next in line for consumption. Provided these are not bruised, they should last for several days – weeks even, in the right conditions – but, even if the blemish is no more than a pinprick or a small bruise, the specimen will not be able to take to long-term storage and, once rotted, will spoil other apples in the store.

Late-keeping apples were kept in baskets lined with well-dried straw, and placed above each other, or laid in heaps on the floor of a loft or anywhere where there was free circulation of air. All fruit, however, must be protected from any sudden changes of temperature. *The Gardener's Assistant* (1859) suggests 'it is advisable to cover them about 1 inch thick [2.5 cm] with straw made very dry by exposure to the sun, or by placing it on kiln. The straw will absorb any moisture that may arise from the fruit, which will ripen of a fair colour and be more plump than if fully exposed to the air . . . they keep very well packed in dry fern, kiln-dried straw, or dry silver sand; they should not, however, be buried in the latter to any great depth, for if almost entirely excluded from the air they lose their flavour.'

Alternately, apples were stored in clean, dry casks: '. . . for packing in these, the apples should be carefully selected, all that are in any way bruised or specked being rejected. After having been in the cask for two or three weeks, it should be opened and the whole picked over, so that any that may then give indications of decay may be removed. Those which do not exhibit symptoms of this process taking place will, on being repacked, keep plump till fit for use, if the cask be put in a dry cool place.'

Pears Pears, with the exception of the earliest varieties such as 'Williams' Bon Chrétien', need to be stored to ripen slowly before they are ready to eat. Traditionally, early pears were stored singly on shelves, while the later were placed in a single layer in drawers or shallow

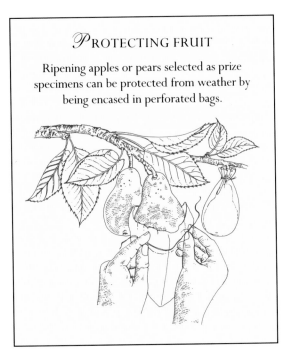

PROTECTING FRUIT

Ripening apples or pears selected as prize specimens can be protected from weather by being encased in perforated bags.

boxes, which ensured a more even temperature. 'Pears keep very well in pure, dry, silver sand, also when packed in kiln-dried straw, or in dried fern,' says *The Gardener's Assistant*.

In the eighteenth and nineteenth centuries large estates had special rooms for storing fruit. Switzer recommended that a fruit room should be '. . . neither a Vault, nor Cellar, nor yet a Garret . . . but let it be a middle Room well ceil'd, and a Place wherein you can make a Fire . . . .' For storing pears, he urged 'use only fine Writing Paper, and every Pear . . . plac'd one by one'. Both pears and apples should be '. . . spread upon dry Wheat Straw or Moss in the Fruitery, or rather as do before directed on Paper, where they should not enjoy much Air, but by all Means keep them from the Frost.' Fruit stored this way should be perfect. If you don't want to use your finest writing paper to wrap the fruit individually, newspaper will do just as well. The wrapped fruit should be laid in shallow boxes or trays in a cool dark place where they will keep for several months. They will need frequent inspections, pulling out any that show the slightest sign of rot.

Preserves

Some of the old preserving techniques are far too good to abandon altogether simply because deep freezing is easier. Bottling fruit, for instance, results in a product range with a completely different set of flavours from those of frozen or canned fruits. Bottled fruits look attractive too, and make delightful gifts. So many pickles and conserves, prepared and packaged in the old ways, enable you to create a fascinating selection of delicacies without having to go anywhere near a supermarket.

VEGETABLES

Vegetables that could not be kept by other means were preserved in salt, particularly runner and French beans. To salt them, the beans were prepared as if for cooking and sliced. About a dessertspoon of salt crushed from block salt was placed in the bottom of a large clean jar with a tightly fitting lid, followed by a layer of beans, then another layer of salt and so on until the jar was filled, finishing with a layer of salt. The lid was screwed on firmly and the jar kept in a cool, dry place. Over the course of a few days the beans would shrink and the jar was then topped up as necessary. When required for the table, the beans had to be thoroughly rinsed in warm water and then soaked in cold water for some hours before cooking as usual.

Cucumbers also keep well in salt. Here is a recipe from Mrs Beetons' *Book of Household*

Management (1861) entitled 'German method of Keeping Cucumbers for Winter use': '*Ingredients*: cucumbers, salt. *Mode*: Pare and slice the cucumbers, sprinkle well with salt, and let them remain for 24 hours; strain off the liquor, pack in jars a thick layer of cucumbers and salt alternately; tie down closely, and, when wanted for use, take out the quantity required, wash them well in fresh water, and dress as usual with pepper, vinegar and oil.'

Shallots and small onions can be pickled, and the following is a recipe from Eliza Acton's *Modern Cookery for Private Families* (1845) for

Before the advent of deep freezes, fruit and vegetables were preserved in glass, a process that imparts a very special flavour to the food.

> **66** *If* you would preserve your Plums with the Blue upon 'em, ... lay 'em ... in a basket among the leaves of Nettles; you must never take them out for fear of rubbing of the Blue.... **99**
>
> London and Wise, 1706

The old-fashioned gardener needed a spacious larder in which to store chutney, jams, raspberry vinegar, pickled onions and other preserves.

FRUIT

Soft fruits were often dried, and the following is the recommended method from Mrs Beeton (1861) for cherries; it would also work for many other soft fruits. First they were put into a slow oven and thoroughly dried until they began to change colour. They were then removed from the oven and tied in bunches and stored away in a dry place; they were used cooked with sugar as a dessert during the winter months. A variation on this was to stone the cherries and place them in a preserving pan, 450 g (1 lb) of cherries to 150 g (5 oz) of loaf sugar strewed over. They were simmered till the fruit shrivelled, then strained and the juice reserved to do another lot of cherries. The cherries were then put in the oven, 'cool enough to dry them without baking them', to dry out.

Bottling fruit was very common in the past and is particularly suited for fruit that does not freeze well, such as pears. One method Mrs Beeton (1861) recommends for bottling fresh fruit is to put the fruit in 'perfectly dry glass bottles', cork the bottles and place them in a very cool oven until the fruit has shrunk away by a quarter, a process that takes 5 to 6 hours! Nowadays, the recommended approach is to use the boiling method for all acid fruits. Here is an adaption of another Beeton recipe 'To Bottle Fresh Fruit with Sugar'. Have some special bottling jars, with new tops, ready in a low oven or covered with hot water. Take any ripe acid fruits, such as currants, strawberries and raspberries, and place them in the jars, discarding any bruised or unripe fruit. Pour over hot sugar syrup (a ratio of 65 ml/2 fl oz sugar syrup to 8 fl oz/250 ml of fruit is about right), making sure that there is a gap of 1 cm (½ in) between the contents and the top of the jar. Seal the jar according to the manufacturer's instructions and place in a bottling kettle or a large saucepan with a false bottom or a wire rack.

pickling both kinds of onions. For pickled onions, boil them a little longer, three to four minutes, until they begin to look clear, and then put the onions into jars and pour the pickle over. She adds that any favourite spices can be added: 'For a quart [1.1 litre/5 cups] of ready-peeled eschalots, add to the same quantity [1.1 litre/5 cups] of the best pale white wine vinegar, a dessertspoonful of salt, and an ounce [25 g] of whole white pepper; bring these quickly to a boil, take off the scum, throw in the eschalots, simmer them for two minutes only, turn them into a clean stone jar, and when they are quite cold, tie a skin, or two folds of thick paper over it.

Obs: The sooner the eschalots are pickled after they are ripe and dry, the better they will be.'

Mrs Acton's recipe was written in the days before food poisoning organisms had been identified. To avoid any problems, nowadays pickled onions should be bottled hot. Spoon the shallots out of the cooking liquid into hot, *sterilized* jars. Bring the vinegar back to a full rolling boil and pour it over the onions, covering them completely and leaving 1 cm (½ in) headspace. Seal immediately. Process the jars for 10 minutes in a boiling water bath or use a steam-pressure canner, following the manufacturer's instructions.

Nasturtium

Make sure that the bottles don't touch the sides or base of the pan or each other – Mrs Beeton suggests placing small hay-wisps round the bottles to prevent them knocking together, but cloths would serve just as well! Pour hot water over the jars to cover them by at least 3 cm (1½ in), bring to a rolling boil and boil for 15 minutes. Remove the jars from the pan and leave them to cool for 24 hours. Make sure that the lids are completely sealed. Store the jars in a cool, dry place.

Right and below: top fruit, soft fruit such as plums and peaches, cultivated raspberries and blueberries and even wild blackberries make a mouthwatering collection whether fresh or preserved.

Pickle is another traditional dish. Here is one of Mrs Beeton's recipes from her American Dishes section (1861): '(*Of Plums, Pears, Peaches, &c.*). *Ingredients*: 7 lbs. [3.2 kg] of fruit, 4 lbs. [1.8 kg] of white sugar, 1 pint [575 ml/2½ cups] of strong vinegar, mace cinnamon and cloves to taste. *Mode*: Pare the peaches and pears, prick the plums, or other fruits, put them in the pan with layers of sugar between the fruit, heat slowly to a boil, add the vinegar and spice, and boil 5 minutes. Take out the fruit with a skimmer and put on dishes to cool, and boil the syrup thick. Pack the fruit in [*sterilized*] glass jars, pour the syrup (boiling) over them and cork tightly.' Nowadays, it is recommended that special bottling jars are used; leave 1 cm (½ in) headspace between the pickle and the top of the jar, seal following the manufacturer's instructions and process the jars for 30 minutes in a boiling water bath (see recipe for boiling fruit).

And finally, here is an intriguing recipe for pickled nasturtiums. *The Gardener's Assistant* tells us that the 'fruits, gathered when green, are pickled in vinegar; and employed instead of capers, to which they are by some considered superior. For this purpose, the second species (*Tropaeolum minus*) is preferred, as it produces more flowers and fruits than the other, and requires no support': '(*A very good substitute for capers*). *Ingredients*: To each pint [600 ml] of vinegar, 1 oz. [25 g] of salt, 6 peppercorns, nasturtiums. *Mode*: Gather the nasturtium-pods on a dry day, and wipe them clean with a cloth; put them in a dry [*sterilized*] glass bottle, with vinegar, salt and pepper, in the above proportion. If you cannot find enough to fill a bottle cork up what you have got until you have some more fit; they may be added from day to day.' The modern equivalent would be to boil and strain the vinegar mixture first, and drop the seed pods into the mixture as they are ready for picking and keep refrigerated.

THE ORNAMENTAL GARDEN

There are many lessons that we can learn from gardens of the past, not only in terms of gardening techniques but also for their designs and decorative ideas. Gardens evolved gradually over the centuries from simple productive sites into places designed for pleasure, and our gardening ancestors experimented over the years with many different plantings and border mixtures – using and discarding countless plant types in order to develop and refine the best plant for flowers, herbs, hedging, and ornamentation, and the most effective design and layout solutions, on both a grand and a domestic scale.

The flower garden

Previous page: an American ornamental garden in the formal style. Detail: delphiniums.

A Pennsylvania farmhouse garden is planted in the cottage style with foxgloves and white irises.

Planting schemes receive far more attention now than they have in the past. This is partly because there are so many plants in cultivation – more than 60,000 frost-hardy species and varieties are grown in the temperate world – and partly because today's garden designs have a greater dependence on plants and plant associations than did those of our forebears. This is particularly so for gardens where naturalistic planting, within a formalized layout, calls for relaxed arrangements of plants, but rigid disciplines in terms of colours, heights and characters of the individual plants. In this way, a kind of symphony or composition is created, using the different foliages, textures and colours in the way that a composer might call on instruments in the orchestra.

To take the musical analogy further, seventeenth-century planting for parterres and knot gardens, with their intricate layout and carefully structured symmetry, was not dissimilar to the baroque and classical harmonies, counterpoint and key systems adhered to by such composers as Handel or J. S. Bach. Edwardian plantings, on the other hand, with their soft romanticism and somewhat undisciplined growth patterns, would be more like the music of Elgar or Verdi, where cold intellectualism has been, at least in part, replaced by a more sensual art form.

Whether you are aiming to re-create the feel and tenor of a specific period, or simply want to make use of the best planting ideas that the past has to give, this chapter offers a retrospective ponder that should provide a rich haul of useful ideas for contemporary gardens.

The medieval physic garden

The monastic physic garden consisted of an enclosed rectangle or a square sparsely planted with a series of small rectangular raised beds filled with dung-enriched soil, whose sides were usually constructed from decay-resisting elm wood planking. Such gardens were always small. The physic garden at Durham, England in the eleventh century, for example, only ran to 30 m (100 ft) by 23 m (75 ft). Raising beds in

Left: herbs such as valerian and feverfew grow in the slightly raised beds of this medieval-style walled garden. When gardens like this were laid out, beauty was not a consideration, but with their symmetry and the changing colours and shapes of the plants, the effect is, nonetheless, delightful.

Below: Bergamot, also known as bee balm or Oswego tea, is a native herb of North America. The scented leaves and flowers are used in tisanes as a digestive, and to give Earl Grey tea its distinctive aroma.

this way enabled soil fertility to be kept at a high level by regular additions of organic material and made it possible to treat different beds in different ways, widening the variety of plants that could be grown.

Neat systems of raised beds can work well in a modern garden and look particularly attractive when their contents, the plants, are spilling over the sides. From the practical point of view, raising the soil surface makes working them easy, and aids drainage on heavy or damp soil. In addition, raised beds enable the gardener to create pockets of different soils, for example for lime-hating plants such as rhododendrons or camellias.

Monks and apothecaries would have grown a miscellany of plants in their raised plots, from ancient roses such as the apothecary's rose (*Rosa gallica*) to the deadly monkshood (*Aconitum napellus*). The monks probably had little regard for the way in which their plants were arranged, but in a modern version of a physic garden there is no reason why you shouldn't indulge in a little artistic licence and enhance the beauty of the design by choosing a tallish shrub for the centre of each bed and arranging the herbs and flowers by colour and character around the sides. The apothecary's rose, for example, looks a delight if surrounded by old clove pinks and the green-flowered lady's mantle (*Alchemilla mollis*). In spring, the same bed could sport cowslips, forget-me-nots and, perhaps, the blue-flowered liverwort (*Hepatica triloba*), which is not to be confused with true liverwort, a non-flowering plant. Bulbs would have been grown here too: squills and crown imperials for medicine and the autumn-flowering saffron crocus (*Crocus sativus*) for the food additive extracted from their stamens. There would also have been lilies, for gracing the altar of Our Lady. The Venerable Bede – an Anglo-Saxon theologian (673–735) – wrote that the white petals of the madonna lily (*Lilium candidum*) represented the purity of Our Lady and the golden yellow anthers were the glowing light of her soul.

Above: sage and cotton lavender (Santolina chamaecyparissus) are traditional knotting hedges. These fragrant shrubs grow quickly, and will produce the desired effect in the shortest possible time.

Below right: of all the Renaissance and sixteenth-century garden design features, the knot garden is the one which most readily lends itself to modern plots, since it can be set to almost any size or scale. .

Hedge shears, 1859

A knot garden

Knot gardens first became popular in the fifteenth century. The early patterns were extremely complicated, with low hedges criss-crossing above and below to give the appearance of threads that have been knotted. The spaces between were filled either with coloured gravels, when they were known as open knots, or with flowering plants, known as closed knots, creating a carpet effect. It is thought that many of the early knot designs were taken from oriental carpets, which had started to arrive in the north via Italy. Such gardens work best on level ground. Planted close to the house, they are as attractive viewed from above as from ground level.

The most appealing aspect of the knot is that, of all period devices, it is the one that best lends itself to modern gardening. Few designs have such a strong, cohesive structure; few make such effective use of a small space. With changing flower colours, making each season interesting, and with aromatic plants which are pleasant to touch and smell, a knot garden will provide perennial enjoyment. The hedging framework is permanent, providing winter outline and disciplining the more exuberant growth of summer. The beds within the hedges offer plenty of scope for ringing the changes and are usually small enough to be easily maintained. Furthermore, a knot garden can be scaled down to fit into the tiniest of modern front gardens.

The choice of plants both for the knot and for the beds within its convolutions needs careful thought, however. Such considerations as year-round interest, minimal maintenance, speed of development and durability of plants all need to be borne in mind. In Elizabethan times, plants were relatively expensive but labour was cheap and plentiful. The reverse is true today.

Skeleton plants for the hedging were traditionally box (*Buxus sempervirens*), yew (*Taxus baccata*), and quicker-growing shrubs such as cotton lavender (*Santolina chamaecyparissus*) or,

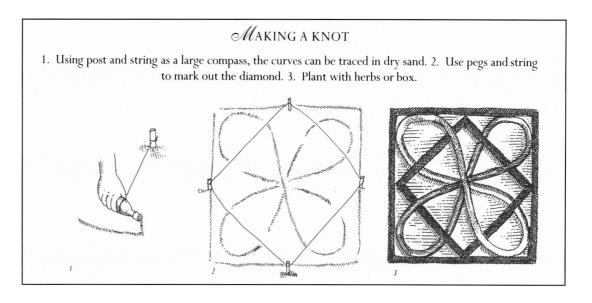

Making a Knot

1. Using post and string as a large compass, the curves can be traced in dry sand. 2. Use pegs and string to mark out the diamond. 3. Plant with herbs or box.

Below: 'Heere I have made the true Lovers Knott To try it in Marriage was never my lott 'Cross Diamonds in the paper I doe frame And in the ground I can draw the same.' Stephen Blake, 1664.

in mild areas, rosemary. Parkinson, in *Paradisi in Sole, Paradisus Terrestris* (1629), complains that cotton lavender is poor in a hard winter, suggesting that it will, 'perish in some places, especially if you doe not strike or put off the snow, before the sunne lying upon it dissolve it', but provided it is clipped hard each year, it will make a useful low hedge for a knot garden in a very short time.

The spaces in between the knotting hedges can be planted formally or informally. Care is needed to select plants which will not grow so vigorously that they invade the hedges, and they must be placed so that they will not overhang any part of it. It is important to try to preserve the outline of the knot so that the planar view is always of a symmetrical pattern.

One useful technique is to fill the spaces created by the hedges completely with ground-cover plants and to trim the tops of these so that they are flush with the top of the hedge. The result resembles carpet bedding and can be made doubly effective if some of the plants flower, creating fields of differing colours. Thus, in a knot of box hedging, the silvery foliage of wormwood (*Artemisia absinthium*) will make a contrasting field which holds its hue for much of the year. A thick planting of annuals

such as vivid blue larkspurs or even bright orange marigolds, or both, will give a flash of brilliance for a few months in summer. These could be preceded by such spring flowers as tulips, florists' anemones or wallflowers, all of which are not only correct for the period but are perfect knot garden plants, being uniform in height, stocky and with good foliage.

Herbs make fine knot garden subjects too. Sage, which comes in purple and golden forms as well as the more familiar green, makes a useful colour contrast and responds surprisingly well to clipping, producing wave after wave of fresh leaves. Marjoram (oregano), especially the golden form, makes an aromatic carpet as does thyme, which should be clipped hard back after flowering to promote healthy young growth. Herbs correct for the period but best avoided in knot gardens include angelica, mint, sweet cicely and lovage. They are all large, invasive plants which need plenty of room. Mint has a creeping rootstock which develops at speed and the others spread their seedlings shamelessly all over the garden. They are, nonetheless, all good and useful plants, providing assorted flavours for the kitchen and looking attractive where they grow – but not in a small knot garden.

Formal bedding plants make a colourful alternative for planting within the hedges of a modern knot garden. Because they merge to make uniform blocks of colour, the style of most would be perfectly in keeping with the knot garden and they are easy to grow from seed – or even easier to buy in the spring as young plants. Some bedding species even pre-date the seventeenth century. A ghost of the Spanish Armada, returning to England today, might look at the planting on Plymouth Hoe and wonder at the petunias and impatiens, but would undoubtedly recognize the French marigolds, and might be able to name the tobacco plants (*Nicotiana*)!

The cottage garden

Up until the nineteenth century cottagers' gardens in country villages were concerned with production of food rather than with beauty. This was to change as landowners were persuaded to demolish the mean housing occupied by their labourers and estate workers and provide them with more spacious plots. The romantic idea of cottage gardening, with roses round the door and a colourful mass of flowering plants in the garden possibly stems from such estate cottages and their improved locations and conditions, and from the wave of gentry in Europe in the eighteenth century who moved to large cottages to live out an idealized rustic lifestyle.

The romantic cottage layout of today still retains many of the original cottage features, including a straight central path leading from the lane to the front door and some kind of boundary hedge, fence or wall with a gateway. An arch over the gateway or porch over the front door overgrown with roses and honeysuckles and perhaps some simple topiary, such as a pyramid or sphere, on either side are also traditional features.

The cottage flower garden is dense and varied, and there are good reasons for this, since it ensures a long flowering season and provides excellent ground cover, which of course also reduces the amount of weeding that needs to be done! In addition, the taller plants will tend to support each other, and will not need extra tying and staking.

Mark Twain's description of Dawson's Landing – a fictitious town just downstream from Saint Louis, Missouri, in 1830 – in *Pudd'nhead Wilson* (1894) illustrates a form of cottage garden and planting that might have applied almost as well to small houses along the Rhine in Europe or colonial cottages in Sydney, Australia: 'Each of these pretty homes had a garden in front, fenced with white palings and opulently stocked with hollyhocks, marigolds, touch-me-nots [impatiens], princes feathers . . . while on the windowsills of the houses stood wooden boxes containing moss-rose plants and terra-cotta pots in which grew a breed of geranium whose spread of intensely red blossoms accented the prevailing pink tint of the rose-clad housefront like an explosion of flame.'

One of the most important contributions the cottager has made to gardens is in the

Right: sage in full bloom, foxgloves blending with old roses, and a wall almost buried under climbing hydrangea make this a model cottage garden.

Below: the essence of the cottage style is to give the impression of random planting, and yet, at the same time, to consider colour and texture and to maintain year-round interest. The annuals in this countrywoman's garden have been planted according to colour and height.

Right: the traditional rose garden, as praised by Dean Reynolds Hole, founder of the National Rose Society of England at the turn of the century, should, strictly, consist of nothing but roses. Less fanatical gardeners, however, prefer to blend their roses with other species. Here, rosemary and other herbs enhance the midsummer display.

Below: old-fashioned climbing roses smother a wall in a fragrant but short-lived burst in early summer.

preservation of many old-fashioned plants that for one reason or another have otherwise gone out of fashion. Cottagers have always enjoyed collecting living curios from the countryside in the form of unusual specimens, and this combined with a loathing to get rid of well-established favourites whatever the latest gardening craze might dictate, has ensured that many flowers, including pinks, primroses and violas, have survived to be discovered afresh by new generations of gardeners.

A garden of old roses

Old-fashioned roses do not belong to any special period. Although a great many 'old' varieties were raised in the nineteenth century, roses have been slipping in and out of cultivation for the last thousand years or more, and many of today's popular cultivars are living antiquities. A great many modern roses are compatible with the older ones too in terms of their colour and character, which allow them

to look comfortable growing alongside their older relatives. There is even a modern nursery breeding a range of brand new 'old-fashioned' roses which combine the ancient characteristics of soft colours and rounded flower shapes with modern attributes of perpetual flowering.

But, in so many respects, the old varieties are the best to grow. Their colours are gentler, softer and more harmonious together than the harsh yellows, salmons and scarlet reds of the modern hybrids. The fragrance of many old varieties is more pervasive than anything being bred today, and varies from the spicy sweetness of the Damask rose to the clean freshness of the climber 'New Dawn'. Disease can be problematic in all hybrid roses, but there is a wide choice of old varieties that, like those bred from *Rosa rugosa*, are resistant to most fungal ills or, like the thornless 'Zéphirine Drouhin', are susceptible but grow so vigorously that they simply shrug the disease off.

For the purist, a rose garden should contain roses and nothing else. Dean Reynolds Hole, an eminent British rosarian of the turn of the century, proclaims rather pompously in *Our Gardens* (1899): 'The Rose Garden must be a garden of roses only. We do not plant shrubs around our oaks, and no birds may warble when the nightingale sings'. But in my view the best rose gardens have always been composed from a miscellany of flowers and foliage arranged to set off the roses to their best advantage.

Timeless classics include *R. mundi* – more correctly *R. gallica* 'versicolor' – whose striped two-tone pink flowers were probably named after 'Fair Rosamond', mistress of Henry II of England. The single-flowered Holy rose

𝒫RUNING STANDARD ROSES

In late winter, the previous season's growth should be cut back to three or four buds from the base of the stem. Try to cut to a bud which faces outwards from the bush. This is also a good time to check ties and post and to replace these if they are worn.

𝒫RUNING CLIMBING ROSES

The optimum time to prune is early winter. The first choice is to select young shoots from the previous season and to tie these in. Older leads which have flowered can then be trimmed of old flower stems and cut back leaving short spurs – each should be cut back to three buds.

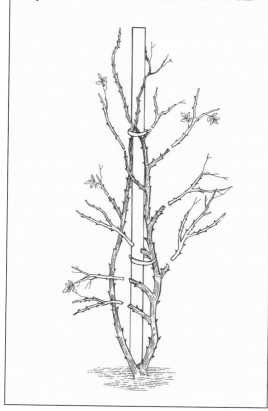

(*R. sancta*) goes back even further and could have been raised in Syria as far back as 300 BC. The moss roses, whose sepals and flower stems are cloaked in a mossy covering, have a special charm, some of them dating back at least to the seventeenth century, and include such varieties as the wine red 'William Lobb' (1855) and the pale pink 'Général Kléber' (1856).

The damask roses were ancient too, and, though only once-flowering, have the sweetest scent and the gentlest pink colour range. 'Ispahan' is one of the most dependable of the damasks and deservedly popular today. The finest blue-green foliage grows on *R. alba* 'Maxima', the Jacobite rose, but of all the alba roses perhaps the most glorious is 'Maiden's Blush', called more daringly by the French 'Cuisse de Nymphe' – thigh of the nymph!

All the foregoing roses can be planted in groups to form the basis of a traditional rose garden. Many of them need only minimal attention and all are tolerant of a wide range of conditions. However, they do all have one large disadvantage: they flower only once in a season.

Cheerfully coloured old-style shrub roses and bright orange eschscholzia liven up this traditional garden.

To overcome the lack of colour after the midsummer flush, a garden of old roses will need an inclusion of more perpetual varieties.

The key to repeat flowering came from the China roses, which were introduced into Europe in the eighteenth century. These provided not only the repeat-flowering habit, but also the genes (exhibited by 'Parks's yellow', 1824) for an extension of the colour range into yellow, with intermediate tones of buff and soft salmon. China roses were used in the breeding of perpetual flowerers such as 'Perle d'Or', which produces an endless succession of exquisite, pointed buds in pale salmon, and the Bourbons, which include the thornless and headily scented, purplish pink 'Zéphirine Drouhin' which is, to this day, one of the world's most popular climbing roses.

The early 1920s saw the arrival of the hybrid musk roses, which provide colour in the autumn. Add a few pure species such as *R. rugosa* and *R. moyesii* to provide autumn hips, and the rose collection is almost complete.

The underplanting is as important as the roses, and should enhance rather than mask their glory. Silver foliage and blue flower colours look sumptuous with old roses, so lavender is a perfect choice, either as edging or to plant in among the roses. Lavender is evergreen and therefore provides winter interest as well. Dark evergreen foliage can be supplied by germander (*Teucrium chamaedrys*) – itself an ancient garden plant – which has pink blossoms that harmonize with the roses. Its shiny leaves look well contrasting with the silver filigree leaves of the wormwood family. Of these, *Artemisia* 'Powys Castle' is one of the most durable and has the most silvery foliage, but as effective ground cover *A. pontica* has the advantage of a creeping rootstock.

Small violas or pansies, particularly in blue and lilac shades, make lowly but colourful companions for roses and flower throughout the growing season, as do the more showy and larger herbaceous penstemons. Hardy cranesbills such as *Geranium himalayense* and *G. pratense* also grace the roses with soft, ephemeral flowers, produced in endless succession, and fine, dissected foliage. For spring, tulips help to extend the season, especially if they are chosen in colours which go well with the reddish emerging leaves of the roses.

The wild garden

Towards the end of the nineteenth century, the wild garden became a popular feature. Far from a wilderness, or an untended spot, the wild garden was, as William Robinson put it in *The Wild Garden* (1894), 'the placing of perfectly hardy exotic plants in places where they will take care of themselves. It has nothing to do with the "wilderness", though it may be carried out in it.' Robinson pioneered this kind of

A century ago, William Robinson encouraged gardeners to grow climbers through trees but warned of the dangers of using too strong a climber for a tree – as here, although the effect is still striking.

gardening, naturalizing a large number of hardy plants in grass or in woodland.

Nowadays, with the natural habitats of so many species under threat, setting up a wild garden can be a way of carrying out a little wildlife conservation in your own back yard. Besides helping to conserve stocks of native plants by growing them at home, a well-balanced wild garden will accommodate a surprisingly wide range of residents and will also attract visiting species.

The secret of success in any wild garden is to get the plants well established to the point where they will form their own self-perpetuating colonies. Initial plantings need to be undertaken with great sympathy for the surroundings, in order to avoid an unnatural or contrived look. Robinson advises: 'All planting in the grass should be in natural groups or prettily fringed colonies, growing to and fro as they like after planting. Lessons in this grouping are to be had in the woods, copses, heaths and meadows, by those who look about them as they go.'

This advice would apply just as well to the flowery mead so beloved of medieval gardeners as to the wild woodland gardens that were created in the nineteenth century. In the wild woodland garden there would be a twisting or meandering path leading through an undergrowth made colourful and interesting with woodland flora planted in naturalistic drifts, such as oxlips, violets, snowdrops, bluebells, and lilies such as *Lilium martagon*, which will rear up above the woodland carpet along with wood cranesbill (*Geranium sylvaticum*).

The wild meadow garden was also a popular item in many Victorian gardens, although they tended to plant non-native British species such as lupins, poppies and geraniums among the grasses. For a more authentic 'flowery meade' that will attract a wide range of wildlife, native meadow wildflowers are best. Unfortunately,

wild meadow gardens are not as easy to establish or maintain as woodland gardens; meadow flowers need a very poor soil (which is not easy to 'create' when you have well-fed garden soil!) and the meadow must be mown only at certain times of the year (depending on the wildflower colonies that have been established) if it is to flower again the following year; a wild woodland garden, on the other hand, will tend to thrive if it is left alone once the initial planting has been done.

Above: water adds another dimension to this wild garden. The structure is naturalistic and the planting random. Such landscapes have been popular since the early 1800s, but more usually on a larger scale.

Left: wild orchids, sorrel, buttercups and mixed meadow grasses thrive in a natural wetland sward such as this, the result of centuries of traditional farming methods.

Above: cranesbills, veronica and a modern shrub rose make a joyful combination of blue and pink in the flower border.

Below: subtle variations on a single colour theme in the Jekyll style, using old roses and pink Pimpinella major *'Rosea'.*

The flower border

The modern flower garden has taken many centuries to evolve to the ideal, naturalistic paradise that is seen at today's fashionable properties. Since around 1900, the individual characteristics of the plants themselves have played an increasingly important role, with careful associations or compositions of different plants making an alternative to massed blocks of the same species. To work effectively, the natural look needs much artifice, with careful attention to the colour, form and texture of plants. The most successful borders will be planted in so relaxed a manner as to approach disorder but will stay this side of chaos, just! Achieving the right degree of informality without the garden becoming dishevelled is difficult to achieve all the time – every garden has its 'off' periods – but should be feasible for much of the year.

Colour, as an abstract concept, did not receive a great deal of attention before the nineteenth century. The English seventeenth-century gardener John Rea, for example, was quite happy to graft several different roses, even in clashing colours, to a single standard stock. But he did recommend giving careful thought to plant associations such as grouping paeonies, tulips and irises together for a spring effect. John Rea's contemporary, Sir Thomas Hanmer, though his garden would have been a formal embroidery of hedges and enclosures typical of the age, also loved certain flowers for their intrinsic beauty, and in particular adored tulips, which he called 'the Queen of bulbous plants.'

But it was the post-1800 gardeners who showed the way as far as successful flower gardening was concerned. The Scotsman J.C. Loudon was a passionate plantsman who, through his prodigious output of reference books and the *Gardeners' Magazine*, encouraged the enjoyment of plants and flowers for their own sakes rather than their massed effect. By today's standards, Loudon's plantings would be considered fussy and self-conscious but, compared with the grandiose schemes of the stately gardens of his day, his concentration on the beauty of the plants was refreshing.

Victorian gardening was rooted in ostentation with loud bedding displays but development of the more naturalistic flower garden gathered momentum again towards the end of the century when William Robinson concentrated his attack on almost every aspect of formal planting in his seminal work, *The English Flower Garden* (1883). Robinson's idea of self-perpetuating colonies of plants grown in grass or woodland to create the perfect wild garden is still relevant today. So too are his recommendations for a high degree of naturalism in more formal surroundings.

The concept of working carefully with colour, however, was crystallized by Robinson's more talented contemporary, the plantswoman and gardening writer Gertrude Jekyll, and it is really thanks to her that the English-style flower garden has become so popular all over the world. About colour and planting, Jekyll wrote: 'Having got the plants, the great thing is to use them with careful selection and definite

Wild European Turk's cap (**Lilium martagon**) *make superb border plants, here enjoying the company of penstemons, mulleins, delphiniums and campanulas.*

Secateurs

Good borders depend as much, these days, on bright foliage as they do on flowers. Here, a variegated willow Salix integra *'Albomaculata' catches the sunlight.*

intention. Merely having planted unassorted in garden spaces, is only like having a box of paints from the best colourman.'

In 1908 Jekyll published *Colour in the Flower Garden*. It would be fatuous to claim that she invented the idea of coordinating colours outdoors, but she *was* the first in recent history to set the concept of colour down in chapter and verse. She stressed the concept that gardening is an art form: 'It is not the paint that makes the picture,' she wrote, 'but the brain and heart and hand of the man who uses it.'

Jekyll's colour plans were, without exception, exquisite, with subtle changes, texture contrasts, and planned succession not so much of continuous flower but of bursts of colour followed by green periods. Her plantings are as desirable today as they were in 1908 in all aspects but one. Belonging, as they do, to an age when skilled labour was inexpensive and readily available, Jekyll did not concern herself with the amount of work and heavy maintenance her schemes required for success. It is possible for modern Jekyll-style flower borders

to adhere to her rules of colour and happy plant association, but they should also be maintainable with less labour.

Here, then, are some ideas for a changing border in the Jekyll tradition. If there is sufficient length – say, 10 m (30 ft) or more – it should not be difficult to arrange for a gentle move through the colour spectrum as one progresses down the border. Thus, if red is selected as the anchor colour in the centre of the border, a move in one direction could run through crimson, magenta, purple, pink and finally to blue, using plenty of variations within this range and lots of foliage to soften the impact of the flowers. Within each colour group, there is scope for further subtle variation. Pink, for instance, could waver to salmon, purple could fade to pale lilac, and white or cream could be used sparingly throughout, just to lighten the effect overall. In the other direction, the red could give way to scarlet, orange and then through ochreous yellow shades to pale lemon, cream or pure white.

Jekyll was keen on contrasts; indeed the most effective way to state a colour more strongly is to contrast it with another. White, for instance, can be used to excellent effect with deep blue. Personally, I have a strong penchant for mixing clean, mid blues with sharp yellows, and for salmon- or apricot-coloured flowers backed up by bronze or coppery foliage.

In reality, a border seldom turns out to be a one-off planned affair. Jekyll fiddled about with hers for forty years! Plants, gifts or impulse purchases perhaps, get popped in, others die or get pulled out. The truly artistic and expert gardener knows just how to place plants with consummate skill and flair. The rest of us trust a good deal more to instinct and, as the more honest will admit, a huge proportion of successful plant association is perhaps no more than good luck!

The rock garden

Like Gertrude Jekyll's plantings, large traditional rock gardens in the nineteenth century took a great deal of looking after and have rather lost favour in private gardens in recent years. The small rockery has, however, continued to delight millions of gardeners all over the world, and although modern collectors are far more careful about conserving the species than were their predecessors of the 1800s, plant-hunting is as popular and widespread as ever, with new species being introduced into cultivation every year.

The stonecrops are almost able to grow in pure rock, eking out a precarious existence on a limited water supply. Many excellent forms of Sedum spurium *have been brought into cultivation, including this one, 'Atropurpureum'.*

In the quest for naturalism during the nineteenth century, the rock garden was a feature that, in the largest of gardens, got grander with each passing year. The *Annals of Horticulture* (1846) illustrates rockwork on some of its pages that would appear to dwarf the alps! There was nothing especially new about the rock garden in the 1830s. The seventeenth and eighteenth centuries had their rustic grottos, and William Forsyth constructed a rock garden – reputedly the first – specifically for growing alpine plants in the Chelsea Physic Garden in London in 1774.

Interest in alpine and rock plants smouldered throughout the last century, but whereas plant hunters were bringing home hundreds of new shrubs and tall herbaceous plants, few small alpine plants were arriving. That changed with one man, Reginald Farrer.

Farrer can, with justification, be dubbed 'the father of the alpine garden'. His love of those small, jewel-like treasures that studded rock and mountain crag was unsurpassed and his descriptions of them, to be found in any of his copious travel books, were in a language more suitable for the heroine of a romantic novel than for plants. This is how he raves about his namesake, *Gentiana farreri*, discovered in the Himalayas: '... each of those weakly stems concludes in the enormous upturned trumpet, more gorgeous than anything attained by *G. gentianella* .... The outline is ... freaked outside in heavy lines of black purple that divide long vandykes of dim periwinkle blue with panels of Nankeen buff between.'

After Farrer came such other Alpine enthusiasts as Walter Ingwersen and Clarence Elliot, who not only collected seed and plants from the wild, but who also multiplied them in their nurseries at home for sale to amateur gardeners all over Britain and, later, to other countries.

The most important aspect of a rockery, regardless of size, or of period, is an authentic

As well as making interesting landscape features, rock gardens also provide planting opportunities for keen collectors of alpines.

appearance. In, regrettably, its most common form, it consists of a mound of earth – perhaps the spoil of a pool dug nearby – with stones pushed into the surface at intervals so that it looks more like an outsize currant bun than a piece of miniaturized landscape. Fewer, larger rocks make a more telling statement than a smattering of small stones. Taking note of the strata – natural layers in the rock – and laying these so that they are parallel helps to create the illusion of a natural crag or mountain side. Using only one kind of rock also helps, especially if it has been extracted locally, and is more desirable than an incongruous mixture. Man-made 'rocks' constructed from plastic or from lumps of concrete are about as convincing and winning as promises from a politician!

As for the planting, it is simply a question of selecting the right plants for the physical conditions and then establishing them in the crevices and pockets between the rocks. Year-round interest is as important on rockwork as anywhere else, and since the great majority of alpines seem to flower either in spring or autumn, those that provide colour at *other* times should be prized.

It is often thought that rockwork needs to be in full sun, but nineteenth-century rockeries and grottos were frequently in shade and therefore depended on plants that throve in cool, shady conditions. Many ferns are happy in gloom, even if fairly dry, and the best of these are evergreen. Hart's-tongue (*Asplenium scolopendrium*) for example is happiest in moist, cool air but with relatively dry feet.

In full sun, the more vigorous rock plants are always in danger of swamping their slower neighbours, so such pretty but exuberant species as *Geranium dalmaticum* need to be carefully policed. Gentler alternatives included *G. farreri*, a plant bearing pretty pink flowers with chocolate stamens. Pinks were also grown in rockwork at the turn of the century, as were a wide

Ormson's jointless tubular greenhouse boiler, 1859

range of primulas, anemones, aubrieta, phlox and helianthemums.

Bulbs, especially small, Mediterranean species extended the season backwards to winter's end. The great British plantsman of the early twentieth century, E.A. Bowles, was an inveterate collector of crocus species, which he grew in his large and constantly expanding rock garden. The earliest flowered with his famous snowdrop collection in midwinter. Others waited until spring, but there were autumn species too.

In autumn, colour can be provided by late-flowering gentians and by such gems from the Mediterranean as the hardy cyclamen species. Of these, the finest foliage belongs to *Cyclamen hederifolium*, but the most delicate of all the flowers belong to *C. cilicium*. Thus, with a microscopic shrub or two – dwarf willow species, perhaps, and *Daphne cneorum* – and with some evergreen foliage supplied by cushion saxifrages and, in the driest spot, sempervivums, the old-fashioned rockery will look interesting every day.

An ornamental conservatory

In the nineteenth century conservatories filled with exotic plants, particularly if they were attached to the house, were usually expected to double as a sitting room where people could bask, alongside the plants, in winter sunlight. The addition of such a 'green room' is equally appealing to many home owners today.

Unless money is no object, the modern conservatory needs to be designed and planted with energy conservation firmly in mind. The hardier the plants, the lower the heating cost will be. Thus, those species that can get through the winter with minimal protection from frost will be the cheapest to maintain. A great many of the conservatory plants that

Far right: with the plant-collecting mania of the nineteenth century, people became fascinated by conservatories. Recently, the conservatory has returned, but modern buildings are designed to be as much an extension of the home as a special structure for displaying exotic and tender plants.

Right: where space is limited, the vinery can double as a conservatory, providing crops of grapes and also somewhere to sit and enjoy a collection of pot plants in a protected atmosphere.

Citrus fruits, perfect for conservatory production in cold climates, make charming feature plants for warmer gardens, having fragrant blossom, fine evergreen foliage and edible fruits.

were beloved in the nineteenth century are perfectly at home in a cool winter where the minimum temperature manages to stay above freezing for most of the time but which may drop close to 0°C (32°F) at night.

Large plants are the most effective if you have the space for them, and can help to create the jungly feel that went with the old conservatories and plantaria. Such traditional conservatory plants as citrus trees have the sweetest fragrance, are evergreen and may even bear fruit. Wattles, particularly the mimosa (*Acacia dealbata*), also have a fresh spring fragrance and feathery foliage which helps to provide dappled shade in summer.

Dramatic summer flowers come from the tree forms of daturas – known more correctly as *Brugmansia arborea* – whose hanging trumpets are often sweetly scented and produced in steady succession. Among herbaceous plants, hedychiums, which are members of the ginger family, have spectacular flower spikes, fresh,

green foliage and a wonderful fragrance. Along with cannas and *Zantedeschia*, they can help to bulk up the luxuriance and create the desired tropic atmosphere.

The crowning glory of any conservatory are the climbing plants. Bougainvilleas, which flower best if starved of water, will quickly swarm up to the highest point and dazzle with their brilliant bracts. Jasmine provides rich scent for much of the year, almost too strong if the windows are closed! Stephanotis and *Hoya*, both popular conservatory plants of antique standing, produce clusters of elegant white flowers, but for today's low-cost building where heat is minimal the New Zealand native *Clematis paniculata* grows vigorously and has waxy white flowers. This is one of the most attractive climbers, but perhaps the most sinister are the climbing birthworts such as *Aristolochia elegans* whose brownish or reddish, speckled, hooded flowers actually give you a start if you come across one of them unawares.

Old-fashioned plants

A mixed border with an old-fashioned blend of shrub roses and dense plantings of herbaceous plants.

*S*ince the majority of garden plants have come to us from earlier generations, the choice of old varieties suitable for modern gardeners is enormous. Look over any garden wall today and you will see that old plants – that is, species or varieties raised more than fifty years ago – will almost always outnumber the more recent cultivars. Among the tens of thousands of varieties available to gardeners, however, there are those extra-special vintage items that have proven, over the centuries, to be so outstanding in terms of form, growth habit, colour and often scent that they have transcended their less distinguished companions and become all-time classics. These are the plants which will be of greatest interest to modern gardeners, especially as many of these tried and tested favourites are, not surprisingly, also easy to grow.

What follows is a selection of plants or plant groups, each of which contains several of these 'premium' varieties and which are still as relevant to our gardens of today, and still as special, colourful, and fragrant, as they were when they first came into cultivation.

ALLIUM

The garlic tribe: onion, garlic, leek, moly.
'In choleric men, it will add fuel to the fire.'
Culpeper, c.1640

By no means restricted to pungent vegetables, this genus of very hardy perennials has no fewer than 450 species, a few of which were grown in ancient times for medicine and food. Fifteenth-century gardeners used the Greek name 'moly' for all of them, although nowadays *A. moly* (H 12–35 cm/5–14 in) refers specifically to golden garlic, a pretty spring bulb with small yellow flowers.

Ornamental alliums are amongst the loveliest summer-flowering bulbs, and many were introduced to Europe during the nineteenth century. Typically, they have drumstick-shaped flowers in various sizes and colours, more commonly in the purple to pink range, but also white and yellow, and include *A. christophii* syn. *A. albopilosum* (H 15–45 cm/6–18 in) and *A. giganteum* (H 1.2–2 m/4–6 ft), both of which are fully hardy and will reproduce freely in well-drained soil in full sun.

AQUILEGIA

Columbine, Granny's Bonnet
'. . . petals . . . like the extended wings of eagle or dove below the spurs of the flowers, which resemble neck and head.' G.S. Thomas, *Perennial Plants*, 1976

The European native, *A. vulgaris* (H 45–90 cm/18–36 in), has been cultivated since the fourteenth century and comes in a delicate palette of blue, mauve, purple, rose and white. It has funnel-shaped flowers with short spurs, unlike some modern hybrids, which have bell-shaped flowers with longer spurs and which offer a wider range of colours. As their natural habitat is open woodland or adjoining

American native columbines such as Aquilegia canadensis *and* A. longissima *have given rise to long spurred hybrids like these.*

meadowland, aquilegias prefer a sunny site with good drainage, and appear from spring through to summer.

New World columbines such as *A. canadensis* (H 30–60 cm/12–24 in) were first brought across the Atlantic by the great plant finder John Tradescant the Younger in about 1640. They display warmer tones of red and yellow and flaunt much longer spurs.

There are many other species of aquilegias, but it is these two that have contributed most to mainstream gardening. Forms of *A. vulgaris* have always been popular in the cottage garden, combining pretty foliage with good blooms and breeding shamelessly to create the self-maintaining colonies so useful to today's naturalistic plantings.

Much work has been done to enlarge the North American *A. canadensis*, elongating its spurs and widening its colour range. The result is a range of gaudy, cheerful border plants, but for sheer elegance and charm, albeit on a subtler scale, the pure American species knock all the fancy hybrids into a cocked hat!

ASTER

Michaelmas daisy, starwort
'There is a quiet beauty about the more select Starworts, which is charming in the autumn days . . .'
William Robinson, *The English Flower Garden,* 1883

The aster is a North American herbaceous species which has given rise to hundreds of excellent garden cultivars, justly prized because they flower with such bright colours so late in the season, providing splashes of pink, lavender-blue or purple in the garden. Alas, many of the older breeds are susceptible to disease, but the strong cadre of exceptions are star performers indeed. *A. novae-angliae* (H 75 cm/2½ ft), which was introduced in 1710, is rather a coarse plant, but its soft clean pink form, 'Harringtons Pink' (H 1.2–1.5 m/4–5 ft), is a treat for early autumn. *A. ericoides* (H 75 cm/2½ ft), which was introduced to Europe in 1732, has several hybrids which produce clouds of tiny starry flowers in pastel shades, and around 1920 the Swiss plant breeder Frikart raised *A.* × *frikartii 'Mönch'* (60–90 cm/2–3 ft), whose large flowers are soft lavender-blue with yellow centres. Asters will grow in any good garden soil in a sunny position, and they can be increased by dividing roots in spring or autumn or by softwood cuttings in spring.

CAMELLIA

'Handsome shrubs of the Tea order.' William Robinson, *The English Flower Garden,* 1883

La dame aux camellias, the consumptive heroine who died in 1852, was following a very widespread fashion when she wore these flowers. Cultivated forms of the shrub *C. japonica* (H 9 m/30 ft) were introduced from China to Europe in the late eighteenth century and by the mid 1880s had become massively popular.

In those days they were grown under glass in Europe, but William Robinson pioneered their culture outdoors during the turn of the nineteenth century and by the 1930s they had become universally popular in the garden, even in cooler climates.

Camellias, especially outdoor varieties, are among the finest of evergreens. The dark green, lustrous foliage, the perfect flower shapes, clean colours (white, and every range of red, from light pink to crimson) and large, perfectly formed blooms give them universal appeal. They do need acid or neutral soil and a sheltered location in areas with freezing winters. Toughest of all, and also among the most decorative, are the 'Williamsii' group raised by crossing *C. japonica* with *C. saluenensis*. Of these, a fine choice would be 'Donation' (H 4 m/13 ft), which has clear pink, semi-double flowers.

*C*AMPANULA
Bellflower

'. . . the most indestructible and amiable of heavy rampers.' Reginald Farrer, 1880–1920, of *C. cochlearifolia*

Campanulas – the name is onomatopoeic – have been grown in gardens for around 500 years. There are many perennial species, from the giant *C. latifolia* (H 1.2–1.5 m/4–5 ft), with clusters of lilac-blue bell-shaped flowers, and stately *C. lactiflora* (H 90–120 cm/3–4 ft), with blue bell-shaped flowers, which were valued for old-style herbaceous borders and are ideal to plant between shrubs in modern mixed plantings, to the tiny *C. turbinata*, whose bold flared flowers on 7.5 cm (3 in) stems will grace the smallest rockery. Some species, particularly *C. rapunculoides*, are invasive and should be avoided. Campanulas will grow in any rich, well-drained soil, in sun or shade. Increase perennials by seed or division in spring.

*C*LEMATIS
Traveller's Joy, Old Man's Beard, Virgin's Bower

'Every gardener loves clematis. I have yet to meet the man or woman that was not attracted by them.' Christopher Lloyd, *Clematis*, 1977

With its huge variation in species, this genus of evergreen or deciduous climbers and herbaceous perennials is the gardener's mainstay when it comes to climbing plants. Ancient in cultivation – it was probably named Virgin's Bower in honour of Elizabeth I of England – and easy to hybridize, it has enabled growers during the last century to provide a rich trawl of superb clematis cultivars. These are increased by taking softwood or semi-ripe cuttings

Above: campanulas were among the first of the alpine plants to be introduced to rock gardens and associate very well, as here, with ferns.

Right: clematis climbing through a lacecap hydrangea.

in early summer; species can be propagated by seed sown in autumn.

Today, the old varieties have never been more popular, since their uses are so varied and their cultivation so simple. Large-flowered hybrids such as *Clematis* × *jackmanii* (H 4.5 m/15 ft), which was introduced in 1858, were bred by crossing the Chinese species *C. lanuginosa* with European natives. Their bell- or flat star-shaped flowers come in a range of colours from deep violet purple, through blue, mauve, pink and white. They are happy growing on walls, on pergolas, through other plants or even over the top of otherwise boring ground-cover plants, in a rich, deep soil with good drainage where their roots are shaded.

The hardy *C. viticella* is itself a delightful European species and has given rise to several charming late-flowering forms, including 'Rubra' (H to 4 m/13 ft), which has red flowers, and 'Alba Luxurians', which has white and green flowers. These can be allowed to swarm over relatively small shrubs, because their trailing stems are cut back every winter.

Oriental species include the orange peel clematis (*C. tibetana*) brought from Central Asia in 1731 and the Chinese *C. tangutica* (H to 6 m/20 ft), a vigorous, late-flowering herbaceous clematis whose lantern-shaped flowers are sharp yellow.

*C*YCLAMEN

'. . . the head or seed-vessel shrinketh downe, winding his footestalke, and coyling it selfe like a cable,' John Parkinson, *Paradisi in Sole, Paradisus Terrestris*, 1629

Wild cyclamen hail from Europe, North Africa and Asia Minor. This Cyclamen hederifolium album *grows freely in much of Europe.*

This tuberous perennial is familiar in most parts of the world as a pot plant, and it derived in the eighteenth century from a species from Asia minor, the fragrant *C. persicum* (H 10–30 cm/4–12 in). With a greenhouse, and a modicum of skill, cyclamen are easy to grow, but, being winter-flowering in the wild, they hate life in most people's living rooms, where the air is too warm.

Hardy species of cyclamen, some of which were cultivated by the ancient Greeks for physic, are easy plants to grow, and are particularly suitable for the modern wild garden, where they give welcome colour in autumn, winter and spring. Toughest is *C. hederifolium* (H to 10 cm/4 in), whose pink or white flowers appear before the foliage. Almost as tough is the midwinter-flowering species from the Greek island of Cos, *C. coum* (H to 10 cm/4 in), which has bright red flowers. Cyclamen prefer well-drained soil and a sheltered position in full sun. They can be grown from seed sown in late summer or autumn.

Dahlia

DAHLIA

'. . . *the most fashionable flower in this country.*' J.C. Loudon, *Encyclopedia of Gardening*, 1829

D. coccinea, the prettiest species in this invaluable genus of half-hardy tuberous perennials, grows wild in Mexico and was brought from there to Spain in 1789. Nurseries soon used it and other species of dahlia to breed a vast range of plants with blooms in almost every colour and size, from tiny pompons to vast decoratives that look more like wedding hats than flowers. There are no true blues, but with that exception every other colour on the spectrum is represented, with the bulk occurring in tones of red, yellow, orange and purple.

Many of the old breeds died out in the second half of the nineteenth century, but by the 1920s there was a vigorous revival. Large exhibition blooms are unsuitable for general garden use, being garish and troublesome to maintain, but there are hundreds of garden varieties which are well worth growing because they provide so much colour so late. One of the finest old breeds to have been revived in recent years is 'Bishop of Llandaff' (H 90 cm/3 ft), whose brilliant scarlet blooms nestle in brooding purple foliage from summer to autumn. Plant dahlias in an open, sunny border in rich,

well-drained soil. To maintain their vigour, dahlias should be propagated regularly, either by seed, basal shoot cuttings or division of tubers in spring. Dwarf forms are grown from seed under glass in late winter.

DENDRANTHEMA

Chrysanthemum

'*These . . . afford a wealth of bloom of diversified colouring when it is much needed in the garden.*' William Robinson, 1883

The habit of botanists to change names of plants may have scientific virtues, but it causes a welter of confusion among practical gardeners. *Dendranthema* is the new name for what almost everyone knows as a chrysanthemum – commonly shortened to 'chrysanth' in England, and 'mum' in North America.

These perennials have been in cultivation for so long that it is difficult to trace and identify the wild species from which they were bred. They figure in ancient Chinese paintings and were probably grown in 500 BC or earlier. They were brought to France in 1789 and shortly thereafter found their way to the rest of Europe and to the Americas.

Old varieties which are of especial merit for modern gardens include 'Emperor of China' (H to 4 m/13 ft) whose silvery pink blooms look all the better for the foliage which reddens in autumn as they emerge. In 1937, Alexander Cumming of Bristol, England, raised the first of the 'Korean' chrysanthemums. These have sprays of small flowers produced late in the season. They are especially useful nowadays, because they are so long-lasting, so vigorous and so easy to multiply. Chrysanthemums will grow in a sunny position in good, well-drained garden soil. Increase by taking basal cuttings in spring. Some dendranthema can be divided in autumn or spring.

Large-flowered dahlia hybrids make splashes of strong colour in the flower border.

DIANTHUS

Pinks, gillyflower, sop in wine, carnations, sweet William

'Queene of delight . . . whose bravery, variety and sweete smell joined together, tyeth every one's affection with great earnestnesse, both to like and to have them.' John Parkinson, 1629

Dating back to the ancient Greeks – Theophrastus coined the name dianthus, which means 'divine flower' – and intensely popular with many fifteenth- and sixteenth-century gardeners, the genus *Dianthus*, which consists of evergreen or semi-evergreen annuals, biennials and perennials, has seen almost as much hybridization and fancy breeding as any of the florists' flowers. The herbalist Gerard and the garden writer John Parkinson both write about carnations and John Rea in the seventeenth century could list 360 different varieties!

The breeding of pinks – rather than carnations – reached the height of its popularity with laced varieties developed by working-class people in Britain in the late seventeenth and early nineteenth centuries.

Many of the old carnations have disappeared, and those that survive are troublesome to manage, but old-fashioned pinks are as easy and gardenworthy as they have ever been. Such centuries-old varieties as the white semi-double and deeply fragrant 'Dad's Favourite' (H 15–30 cm/6–12 in) with chocolate-brown lacing, 'Paisley Gem' (H 15–30 cm/6–12 in), and the deep maroon, silver-lined 'Camilla' (H 15–30 cm/6–12 in), are deservedly popular plants today.

Besides pinks and carnations, there are some 300 species of dianthus growing wild in Europe, Asia and Africa, but relatively few have been exploited by our forebears. The maiden pink (*D. deltoides*) is one exception which still makes an excellent plant for the rock garden, but perhaps the most popular species, after the

true pinks and carnations, is the sweet William (*D. barbatus*), which makes a superb cut flower as well as a fine garden plant (H 30–60 cm/12–24 in). Any good rich garden soil will do for dianthus; they need a sunny position in the border. Increase by seed in late spring.

Garden pinks, raised from several wild species of dianthus, are a mainstay of the traditional garden. They thrive on an alkaline soil and dislike extreme damp conditions.

FUCHSIA

'Graceful and distinct shrubs, flourishing near coasts, ...' William Robinson, 1883

One of the world's most popular plants, fuchsias originate from Central and South America and were brought into cultivation by the nineteenth-century English nurseryman James Lee, who is said to have spotted a fuchsia, brought home as a curio, growing in the window of a sailor's cottage in Wapping,

Fuchsia

London. He bargained with the sailor's wife and from this original plant rooted some 300 softwood cuttings (fuchsias can be increased in any season by this method).

Other fuchsia species soon followed and, after much hybridization, the fuchsia still stands unsurpassed as a container plant for summer colour. Old varieties offer few advantages over modern ones, but of the original species the deciduous *F. magellanica*, lady's eardrops, remains a firm favourite. It is almost frost-hardy and will grow into a large straggling shrub (H 3 m/10 ft) in mild areas in a sheltered position in a rich, moist soil. Its small tubular blooms are a charming blend of blood-red and navy blue and offers wonderful opportunities as it is seldom out of flower.

$\mathscr{G}$ALANTHUS
Milk flower, snowdrop

'. . . a most graceful dangling thing, flowering later than the little Galanthus nivalis.' Reginald Farrer, 1880–1920, of G. elwesii

Natives of central and southern Europe, snowdrops have been collected by keen plantsmen since Edwardian days. There's even a term for such enthusiasts – 'galanthophile'. Originally, of course, species were collected from the wild, but today such practices are illegal, and unnecessary, since plentiful stocks are raised commercially by specialist nurseries.

There are several hundred forms to collect, though spotting the differences between some varieties needs the aid of a magnifying glass and a fertile imagination! Exceptional clones, however, include 'Atkinsii' (H 10–25 cm/4–10 in), named in 1875, which flowers in late winter and early spring, the outsize 'Sam Arnott', which grows 15 cm (6 in) taller than any other snowdrop, and the 1876 introduction, *G. nivalis reginae-olgae*, (H 10–20 cm/4–8

in) the autumn snowdrop, named after Queen Olga of Greece, which, not surprisingly given its common name, flowers in autumn rather than late winter. Snowdrops thrive in a cool, shaded position and a rich, moist garden soil. Divide in spring after flowering.

$\mathscr{G}$ENTIANA
Gentian

'. . . every day . . . brings a fresh crashing explosion of colour in the fold of the lawns.' Reginald Farrer, 1880–1920, of G. farreri

Much romance has been attached to this bluest of flowers, whose azure phonograph-shaped trumpets grace the upland grasses, not only of the Swiss Alps but also of the Himalayas.

Many of the more exquisite varieties collected by Farrer and his contemporaries – and hybridized by such renowned alpinists of the first half of the twentieth century as Clarence Elliot – are plants with exacting requirements. The most notable exceptions are the perennial spring-flowering European *G. acaulis* (H 2–7.5 cm/¾–3 in) and the Asian summer-blooming *G. septemfida* (H 15–25 cm/6-10 in). The latter is an evergreen perennial and prefers humus-rich soil which stays moist, but the former seems to tolerate almost any conditions. Divide or sow seed in autumn.

Left: the double form of the common snowdrop, Galanthus nivalis; snowdrops are best grown in large drifts in shade where they can naturalize.

Below: spring-flowering gentians from Europe were grown for centuries before the plant hunters discovered the many lovely autumn-flowering species in the Himalayas. This is a form of Gentiana septemfida which flowers towards the end of the summer.

Gentian

GERANIUM
Cranesbill

'They fit into their surroundings with that subtle sympathy which weds the harebell to the heaths.' A.T. Johnson, 1873–1956

As meadow and woodland wildings, geraniums were popular with such naturalistic gardeners as Gertrude Jekyll and William Robinson. Their easy culture – they will grow in almost any soil that is not too wet, in sun or partial shade – and quiet beauty make them perfect subjects for today's gardens, whether as hardy perennial groundcover between shrubs or as components of a wild garden in summer. Most species are gardenworthy and what little hybridization that has taken place has provided some fine cultivars, including the lovely lavender-blue 'Johnson's Blue' (H 30 cm/12 in), which retains the wild charm of both its parents, *G. pratense* (H 75 cm/2½ ft) and *G. himalayense* (H 30 cm/12 in). Divide or grow from seed in autumn or early spring.

GLADIOLUS
Sword lily

'Those who desire their gardens to be beautiful late in the autumn should not fail to employ the Gladiolus largely.' William Robinson, 1883

When the Scottish plant hunter Francis Masson visited South Africa in 1772, he brought home a wealth of valuable plants including 50 species of pelargoniums and a huge number of bulbous species, including the non-European corm *Gladiolus*. These became florists' flowers and in subsequent eras were bred to heights of vulgarity. Original species – such as the pink and green *G. papilio* syn. *G. purpureo-auratus* (H 90 cm/3 ft) and soft yellow *G. primulinus* (H 90 cm/3 ft) – are currently enjoying a well-deserved revival in popularity. In well-

sheltered, sunny gardens, they make a huge contribution, stretching summer into autumn. Gladioli can be propagated by seed if sown in early spring in a cool greenhouse, or from offshoots which can be planted out in spring. Mature corms are widely available for planting in spring.

IRIS

'. . . in full glory, in the middle of May, it is as beautiful as anything in the garden.' E.A. Bowles, writing about his iris bed, *My Garden in Spring*, 1914

The iris is one of the oldest plants in cultivation. Orris, an ancient herbal preservative and perfume, is made from the roots of *I. florentina*, and the French heraldic *fleur-de-lys* – dating back to the sixth century – is a depiction of the iris flower.

During the last two centuries, breeders and collectors have created a vast range of irises suited to almost every aspect from arid to aquatic. For moisture-loving plants, the Japanese-bred *I. ensata* syn. *I. kaempferi* (H 60–90 cm/2–3 ft) are best, with their huge, flat flowers in pastel colours, but in a mixed border older varieties of the rhizomatous *I. sibirica*, such as 'Heavenly Blue' (H 90 cm/3 ft) and 'Emperor' (H 90 cm/3 ft), flower much more freely than their modern counterparts in early summer. Most of the bearded irises are best in sun in well-drained soil, but, sadly, many of the old hybrids have been ousted by more garish modern varieties. However, orris and the other species used to breed modern bearded hybrids, namely the yellow *I. variegata* (H 30–50 cm/12–20 in) and the scented lilac-blue *I. pallida* (H 70-90 cm/28–36 in), have long been in cultivation and make enchanting garden plants. Propagation of rhizomes is by division immediately after flowering.

Iris sibirica, *hardy and vigorous, is a perfect border plant.*

ℒILIUM
Lily

*'Have you seen but a white lily grow
Before rude hands have touched it?'* Ben Jonson,
1573–1637

The Madonna lily (Lilium candidum) is one of the oldest flowering plants in cultivation. The flowers are strongly fragrant and, uniquely among lilies, the first foliage emerges in autumn.

Another vast group of mainly summer-flowering bulbs, ranging from the short-stemmed *L. nanum* (H 15–45 cm/6–18 in) to the stately *L. candidum* (H 60–90 cm/2–3 ft), the madonna lily. This fragrant white lily is one of the oldest recorded plants, possibly grown as a

food plant before Christian times. Its scent and hardiness make it a lasting favourite.

Asian lilies, collected by such naturalists as George Forrest and Ernest Wilson from China at the turn of the century, have been developed into a huge range of cut-flower plants as well as garden perennials. Some of these modern hybrids are susceptible to a debilitating virus, but many original species, particularly the orange-red *L. lancifolium* (H 60–150 cm/2–5 ft), the tiger lily, and the soft-apricot *L. henryi* (H 90–300 cm/3–10 ft) seem either resistant or able to survive the disease. Propagate by seeds in autumn or spring, or by bulb scales just after flowering. Most lilies will grow in any good garden soil in a sunny position.

ℳAGNOLIA

'The most sumptuous, sculptured flowers of any hardy tree or shrub, often coupled with fine texture, rich colour and fragrance.' G.S. Thomas, *Ornamental Shrubs, Climbers and Bamboos*, 1992

Among the first of the flowering plants, magnolias have been found fossilized from over five million years ago. Their culture in Western gardens is rather more recent, however, and appears to be rooted in France. One of the first in cultivation was the American evergreen species, *M. grandiflora* (H 9 m/30 ft), introduced to the Old World in the early eighteenth century and named after the French botanist Pierre Magnol, who died in 1715. The most popular hybrid, however, is the hardier deciduous *M.* × *soulangeana* (H 6 m/20 ft), which bursts into white tulip-like flowers flushed with purple in mid-spring until early summer. The offspring of two Chinese species which occurred by chance at the château of Soulange-Bodin in France in 1826, it was soon to become widespread and is still a compact enough tree to make a perfect modern plant with a rich

Magnolia

The deciduous Magnolia × soulangeana flowers young and looks lovely in spring underplanted with grape hyacinths (Muscari sp).

fragrance. Even more compact is the smaller, star-shaped flowered deciduous *M. stellata* (H 2.7 m/9 ft), the star magnolia, introduced from Japan in the 1870s. Magnolias prefer a sheltered position, and most will grow in a well-cultivated, well-drained soil, although some species thrive best in a slightly acid soil. Propagate from freshly collected seed in cool compost, or by layering in summer or autumn.

NARCISSUS
Daffodil, jonquil, Lent lily

'Fair daffodils we weep to see
You haste away so soon!
As yet the early-rising sun
Has not attained his noon.' Robert Herrick, c.1648

Few genera have been developed to such a diverse range of shapes and sizes and, in spite of Herrick's lament, part of their charm is that daffodils are here today, gone tomorrow. Despite the efforts of hybridizers over the ages to produce pink or red blooms, colours tend to stick in the golden or white range. The reddest hue is seen in the tiny eye of the fragrant *N. poeticus* (H 23–42 cm/9–17 in), the pheasant eye

or poet's daffodil, but there are trumpet daffodils such as 'Passionale' (H 40 cm/16 in) which have white petals and a pinkish cast to their trumpets instead of the more usual yellow. Bulb catalogues and garden centres burgeon with dry bulbs on offer every autumn, their promises of a garish display backed up by larger-than-life colour pictures. But so many of the old hybrids and species are so much more dependable, being more natural-looking and quicker to multiply than many of the larger flowered cultivars.

Among white narcissus, *N. poeticus* 'Recurvus' (H 42 cm/17 in), the true pheasant eye, flowers in late spring and has a delicious fragrance. The yellow daffodils which inspired the nineteenth-century poet Wordsworth when he saw ten thousand at a glance, fluttering and dancing in the breeze in the English Lakeland, were *N. pseudonarcissus* (H 15–30 cm/6–12 in), the Lent lily or wild daffodil. This low-growing species is ideal for planting in masses beneath mature trees where, if happy, it will seed itself liberally, building up stocks over the years. Narcissi will grow in any well-drained soil in sun or light shade. Propagate from fresh seed in autumn.

PAEONIA
Paeony

'They all have great beauty of leaf and flower, but look rather gaunt . . . in winter.' G.S. Thomas, 1992

In 1925 the American plant collector Joseph Rock gathered seeds of a moutan or deciduous tree paeony from a monastery – or, more technically, a lamasery – in Kansu, Tibet. He sent seed back to the Arnold Arboretum in the United States, whence it was distributed to a few selected growers. Known as *P. suffruticosa* 'Rock's Variety' (H to 2.2 m/7 ft), the huge

Brought to Europe from Asia in the late eighteenth-century, the herbaceous paeony, Paeonia lactiflora, was bred to produce a vast range of garden varieties with huge flowers, many of which are sweetly scented.

cup-shaped flowers are pure white with a maroon base to each petal and, once seen, are quite unforgettable. Sadly, it has never been re-discovered in the wild and is slow to propagate, but fortunately it is only one of a large number of deciduous tree paeonies. Their flowers range in colour from deep wine red through pink to white, and there are also yellow tree paeony hybrids and a number of distinctive woody species.

Most herbaceous paeonies were raised from the Chinese species *P. lactiflora* (H to 90 cm/3 ft) and the number of old varieties still in general cultivation demonstrates what a dependable plant this is. William Robinson (1883) listed more than sixty. Of these, the white double 'Festiva Maxima' (H 90 cm/3 ft), soft pink 'Madame Calot' (H 90 cm/3 ft) and deeper 'Glory of Somerset' (H 90 cm/3 ft) are still widely available.

The European *P. officinalis* (H to 60 cm/2 ft), grown as a medicinal plant by European medieval monks, makes a fine flower for the spring garden, particularly in its double forms. Few varieties have survived other than a deep rose red and a near white. Paeonies prefer a sunny location and a rich, well-drained soil. Perennials can be grown by seed or by division in autumn or early spring.

$\mathscr{P}$APAVER

Poppy

'On a half reaped furrow sound asleep.
Drowsed with the fume of poppies, while thy hook
Spares the next swath and all its twined flowers.' John Keats, 1795–1821, *To Autumn*

A vast group of garden plants, the poppy family includes vibrant tones of field poppies, oriental perennial kinds, and the glaucous-leafed *P. somniferum* (H 75 cm/2½ ft), the opium poppy. Without exception, this is a beautiful family, its only fault being fecundity!

The scarlet field poppies, with their mixed imagery of sleep and of war, add blotches of vermilion to the summer border, but in 1880 the Reverend Wilks, of Shirley, England, spotted a pale freak poppy and used this to breed one of the finest strains of fast-growing hardy annuals, the Shirley poppy, *P. rhœas* (H 60 cm/2 ft). Their lemon stamens and pink coconut-ice flowers, produced in constant succession throughout the growing season, make them perfect for any garden where there is a sunny site where they can be left to self-seed.

$\mathscr{P}$ELARGONIUM

Pot geranium

'Pelargoniums require a great deal of air . . .'
Mrs Loudon, *Gardening for Ladies*, 1846

The Scottish plant hunter Francis Masson collected no fewer than 50 species of pelargonium on his trips to South Africa in the late

Right: perennial phlox provides a succession of clean pink fragrant blooms which are especially popular for flower arranging.

eighteenth century. These formed the basis for one of the most useful ranges of tender summer-flowering perennials in cultivation. Constantly in flower, easy to cultivate and as happy in formal plantings as in more naturalistic displays, pot geraniums come near to being indispensable. Many have brilliantly coloured flowers, others have shapely, aromatic foliage.

A high proportion of modern pelargonium hybrids are raised from seed and come in a wide range of colours, many of them uncomfortable on the eye, or worse, in washy pastel shades hardly suited to their characters. However, many of the old varieties are available, either with true geranium-red flowers or with aromatic foliage, and are still deservedly popular. Cleanly marked foliage on such evergreen pelargonium varieties as 'Dolly Varden' (H 30 cm/12 in) and the trailing 'Elégante' (H to 60 cm/2 ft) make them especially good. Among scented leaf forms, 'Paton's Unique' (H 60 cm/2 ft) combines deeply cut, fragrant leaves with brilliant pink blooms. They are all easy to grow from cuttings from spring to autumn. As bedding plants, pelargoniums need a sunny site and well-drained soil.

Below: penstemons were introduced to Europe from North America in the late eighteenth century, and are invaluable in the herbaceous border with their deep, rich colours and long flowering.

$\mathcal{P}$ENSTEMON

'. . . *their beauty covers five months, commencing . . . with the charming blue* P. procerus, *and finishing with the endless varieties of* P. hartwegii *in shades of rose, scarlet and crimson, whose beauty holds its own even in November, after more fragile plants have perished.'* William Robinson, 1883

Penstemons are herbaceous and shrubby species from the New World, whose trumpet flowers are of great beauty with a full range of colours, both warm and cool. The two species that have given rise to the most useful hybrids are the Mexican semi-evergreen *P. campanulatus* (H 30-60 cm/12–24 in), introduced in 1794,

and *P. hartwegii* (60 cm/2 ft), brought into cultivation from Mexico a quarter of a century later. Tough varieties such as the midsummer to autumn flowering pale pink 'Evelyn' (H 45 cm/18 in) and red 'Garnet' (H 60-75 cm/2–2½ ft) were raised from these species and are almost hardy except in severe frost. Penstemons prefer a sunny border and rich, well-drained soil. Propagate by seed in early spring, or from young cuttings in midsummer.

$\mathcal{P}$HLOX

'As plants go, Phlox $\times$ decussata *is one of the easiest to grow and will put up with most conditions of soil and aspect as well as treatment.'* H. Symons-Jeune, *Phlox*, 1954

Phlox is a genus of North American herbaceous and alpine plants of the Jacob's ladder family which comes in a range of clean, bright colours and has many uses in the garden. Modern hybrids raised from the perennial *P. paniculata* (H 1.2 m/4 ft), introduced in 1730, tend to come in loud, garish colours and are susceptible to eelworm (nematodes) and mildew disease.

Descendants of the perennial *P. maculata* (H 90 cm/3 ft), introduced in 1740, are smaller, more refined perennials with glossy foliage and great staying power. The pink 'Alpha' (H 45 cm/18 in) and 'Omega' (H 90 cm/3 ft), which is white with a carmine eye, are two hybrids still available and worth looking for. One of the finest single perennial phloxes is the stalwart, pure white 'Mount Fuji' (H 1.2 m/4 ft). These phloxes can be increased by seed in autumn or spring, or by division in early spring or by root cuttings in winter. Phloxes prefer full sun and they need a fertile, well-drained soil.

PRIMULA

Primrose, cowslip, auricula

'The cowslips tall her pensioners be:
In their gold coats spots you see;
Those be rubies, fairy favours,
In those freckles live their savours:
I must go seek some dewdrops here
And hang a pearl in every cowslip's ear.'
Shakespeare, *Midsummer Night's Dream*, 1595

Not a large family but of immense value to gardeners since medieval times. The sixteenth-century herbalist John Gerard praises the pale native British primrose and in the seventeenth century John Rea declares that 'were it not so common in every Country woman's garden it would be more respected.' Much later, in the nineteenth century, the more exotic forms of primrose, polyanthus and also of *P. auricula* were developed. Many are still in cultivation and make fine spring plants. Of especial note are the double lilac primrose *P. vulgaris* 'Lilacina Plena' (H 15–20 cm/6–8 in), known since the 1600s, and the maroon-laced polyanthus strains of the nineteenth century. Both make handsome plants in a sunny or partially shaded border and can be multiplied by division.

Primulas collected from the Asian uplands have contributed much to the gardeners' repertoire of moisture-loving herbaceous perennials. Most of them come in bright, clean colours and are easy and dependable from seed. The giant *P. florindae* (H 60–90 cm/2–3 ft), the Himalayan cowslip, was introduced by the English plant hunter Frank Kingdon Ward and will self-sow where summers are cool and moist.

RHODODENDRON

'It must indeed be confessed that some of our floral favourites are fastidious in their diet.' Dean R. Hole, *Our Gardens*, 1899.

This is a huge group of evergreen, semi-evergreen and deciduous plants, which requires neutral to acid soil to thrive. Probably the best known collector of rhododendrons was Joseph Hooker (1817–1911), but there were many others. Rhododendrons – and the genus includes azaleas – became something of an obsession with the world's more influential gardeners from the 1850s onwards. Hybridization and selection was carried out at many of the grander residences, giving rise to vast shrubs which needed acres in which to grow, and which were spectacular for a couple of weeks in spring, but boring for the rest of the year with their sombre, drooping foliage.

For modern gardeners, especially if space is limited, there are plenty of small rhododendrons which have their place, even though their flowering season may not be very long. Small species such as the evergreen *R. yakushimanum* (H 90 cm/3 ft) are best for small gardens because they have attractive foliage as well as flowers. Other small hybrids include *R.* 'Blue tit' (H 90 cm/3 ft) and the scarlet evergreen *R.* 'Elizabeth' (H 1.5 m/5 ft). Apart from a lime-free soil, they prefer a cool, moist and humus-rich soil. Increase by semi-ripe cuttings or layering.

Rosa *'Juane Desprez'*

Rosa *'Village Maiden'*

Primula

$\mathcal{R}$OSA

Rose

'Le lion est toujours le roi des animaux, l'aigle le monarque des airs, et la Rose la Reine des fleurs.'
Redouté, 1759–1840
(*The lion is ever king of the animals, the eagle lord of the air, and the rose queen of the flowers.*)

The rose is the mainstay of the temperate garden, with thousands of varieties providing plants suitable for almost every aspect except deep shade. Among the old breeds, a common problem is a limited flowering season. Few people find this a negative feature in rhododendrons or lilacs, but, because so many modern roses repeat, those that do not are discriminated against. Here is a tiny selection of old roses that are dependable, easy plants and therefore as perfect for the modern garden as they were when they first appeared.

Pre-1880s non-repeating roses These include the white centifolia *R.* 'Mme Hardy' (H 1.5 m/5 ft); *R. gallica* (H 1.5 m/4 ft), the apothecary rose, with plummy red flowers, and 'Rosa Mundi' (H 1 m/3½ ft), with two-toned striped flowers; the Damask pale pink, deeply fragrant 'Isaphan' (H 1.5 m/5 ft), which is probably the most widely available; and the white Alba *R. alba* 'Maxima' (H 2.2 m/7 ft), and the *R. alba* 'Queen of Denmark' (H 1.5 m/5 ft).

Post-1800 repeating roses These include the China 'Old Blush China' (H 90 cm/3 ft), which has double, warm pink flowers; the salmon-pink China 'Perle d'Or' (H 75 cm/2½ ft); and the pale pink China 'Cecile Brunner' (H 75 cm/2½ ft). From the Bourbon species there is 'Honorine de Brabant' (H 1.8 m/6 ft), which has two-tone striped mauve to pink flowers. The Hybrid Musks offer a wide range. There are the scented, pale salmon 'Penelope' (H 1.5 m/5 ft); the slightly fragrant, apricot-coloured 'Buff Beauty' (H 1.8 m/6 ft); the white 'Pax' (H 1.5 m/5 ft); the lemon to white 'Prosperity' (H

1.2 m/4 ft); and the red 'Will Scarlet' (H 1.2 m/4 ft). Among the Spinosissima there are the white 'Stanwell perpetual' (H 1.8 m/4 ft), and 'William the Third' (H 75 cm/2½ ft), which has fragrant deep pink flowers and ferny foliage. From the old ramblers, the scented, salmon-pink 'Albertine' (H to 5 m/16 ft); the creamy 'Rambling Rector' (H 6 m/20 ft); and the white 'Felicite Perpetue' (5 m/16 ft) are all popular. Old climbers include the thornless 'Zéphirine Drouhin' (H to 2.5 m/8 ft), which has lilac-purple to pink scented flowers, and the thornless Bourbon 'Kathleen Harrop' (H 2.5 m/8 ft), which has pale pink flowers. Rugosa roses are the most disease-resistant and include the pale yellow 'Agnes' (H 1.2 m/4 ft); the strongly scented, wine-red 'Roseraie de l'Hay' (H 2.2 m/7 ft); the single pink 'Frau Dagmar Hastrup' (H 1 m/3½ ft); and rich cerise to red 'Mrs Anthony Waterer' (H 1.5 m/5 ft), which has a tiered habit.

Most roses prefer an open, sunny site and rich, heavy, well-drained soil which stays moist. They can be increased by budding in summer or by hardwood cuttings in autumn.

'Souvenir de la Maison', an old Bourbon rose raised in 1843, has the soft colouring and distinctive charm sadly lacking in most modern breeds.

Gallica rose

China rose

Old-fashioned China roses in an open setting.

Above: pansies have been in cultivation for hundreds of years. They come in a vast range of sizes and colours and are easy to raise from seed.

Top: formal spring bedding, here with orange tulips and blue Universal Pansies, began to appear in the 1840s and soon became extremely popular.

TULIPA
Tulip

'The Queen of bulbous plants, whose flower is beautiful in its figure, and most rich and admirable in colour.' Sir Thomas Hammer, 1612–1769

Tulips originate from the Middle East, and graced Arab gardens for centuries before being introduced to the palaces of European royalty. The Frenchman Charles L'Ecluse (1526–1609), who was also known as Clusius, is said to have brought them to Holland where they may have formed the basis of the Dutch bulb industry. He has *T. clusiana* (H to 30 cm/12 in), the lady tulip, a fine garden-worthy species named after him. This is still grown commercially.

Modern hybrid tulips, for all their size and brightness, are no better than the older varieties, several of which have survived for centuries. The red of the old 'Couleur Cardinal' (H 40 cm/16 in), for example, is stronger than anything bred today and looks wonderful with the closely related orange and tan 'Princess Irene' (H 40 cm/16 in). Both varieties have dark foliage which complements the flower. 'Apeldoorn' (H 60 cm/2 ft), more recent but still relatively old, is a top seller, as is the pearly pink cottage tulip named 'Clara Butt' (60 cm/2 ft) after one of the most distinguished contraltos of a previous generation. Tulips prefer a sunny position and well-drained soil; increase your stock by dividing bulbs in autumn.

VIOLA
Violets, pansies, violettas

'No race is more fertile or of more exquisite beauty, ...' Reginald Farrer, 1880–1920

Violets are a lowly but valuable race of plants which includes a few spectacular varieties but depends more on massed blooms, or discreet charm, to win gardeners over.

Among old varieties, the saddest event has been the steady dying out of the best sweet violet cultivars as the fashion to give and receive bunches of their flowers has disappeared. Many of these are fussy to grow but are exquisitely scented. One great exception is *V.* 'Amiral Avellan' (H 10 cm/4 in), a fragrant garden violet that grows with vigour and thrives on neglect.

Florists' pansies, with their comic faces, are hard to take seriously these days, but they have evolved into the most useful garden plants, being easy to cultivate and flowering almost all year. Smaller flowered violas date from the 1860s, and are the result of breeding experiments carried out by James Grieve. He crossed the rhizomatous perennial *V. cornuta* (H 12–20 cm/5–8 in), the beautiful horned viola – itself a fine garden plant – with *V. lutea* (H 10 cm/4 in), the mountain pansy, to produce a fine, long-lasting range of colourful, low-growing perennial plants for summer. Of these, the best today include the light mauve *V.* 'Maggie Mott' (H 15 cm/6 in); *V.* 'Irish Molly' (H 10 cm/4 in), which has odd khaki and greenish-yellow flowers; and the enchanting chocolate and yellow bicolour *V.* 'Jackanapes' (H 7.5–12 cm/3–5 in), named by Gertrude Jekyll.

All these violas seed freely and will make self-maintaining colonies, flowering best when cut back every few weeks to promote new growth. Few plants are better natured, and will grow in sun or shade and well-drained but moist soil.

Ferns
Ferns cover a large group of non-flowering plants, which were adored by nineteenth-century gardeners but slipped into decline with the coming of the twentieth century. Sadly, many fine garden forms of ferns were lost – a great pity for such tolerant, manageable plants.

A large number of ferns are fully hardy and drought-resistant provided they do not have too much direct sunlight. Aquilegia, serastrum and fern make a fine association in gentle shade.

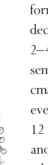

Maidenhair fern

Their cool, pale green, feathery foliage and graceful habits make them ideal for the shady part of a modern mixed border, where they make a lacy background to more colourful flowering plants. Ferns are also natural companions to one of the most popular 'modern' foliage plants, the hostas (*Hosta* sp.), helping to melt away the too-solid flesh of the hosta foliage with their dainty fronds.

Pure species of ferns with pretty garden forms for the moist, shaded garden include the deciduous *Athyrium filix-femina* (H 60–120 cm/ 2–4 ft), the delicate, arching lady fern; the semi-evergreen *Asplenium trichomanes* (H 15–30 cm/6–12 in), the tiny maidenhair fern; and the evergreen *Polypodium vulgare* (H 25–30 cm/10– 12 in), the common polypody. *A. filix-femina* and *A. trichomanes* can be propagated by spores when ripe in late summer. Divide *P. vulgare* in spring, or propagate by spores in late summer.

For wet, semi-shaded positions, there are two classic deciduous ferns: the ostrich or ostrich-feather fern (*Matteuccia struthiopteris*) from North America, which gives great service after more than 200 years in cultivation (H 2 m/6½ ft), and *Osmunda regalis* (H 2 m/6½ ft), the royal fern, perhaps the largest and most handsome fern, and one that occurs wild on most continents. Both can be divided in autumn or winter or grown from spores when ripe.

Old-fashioned conifers

This huge group of trees and shrubs which includes cedars, larches, pines, spruces, firs and cypresses, has played such an important role in horticulture over the last couple of millennia that it is hard to imagine ornamental gardens without them. The great majority are evergreens whose foliage is either in the form of tiny scales or 'needles'. They occur in many parts of the world but are especially abundant in the cooler regions of the northern hemisphere. Many have been in cultivation, or used in forestry, for so long that it is easy to forget the brave souls who discovered and took them from one part of the world to another. The intrepid nineteenth-century Scottish plant hunter, David Douglas, for example, has the North American Douglas Fir (*Pseudotsuga taxifolia* syn. *P. Douglassi*) named after him.

During the twentieth century, with a steady reduction in garden size and a growing demand for dwarf and slow-growing forms, the number of smaller garden varieties increased. Recent history has seen the proliferation of a huge range for dwarf forms – often of a freakish nature – whose growth is more restrained than that of their parents. These varieties are perfect for small gardens, and include *Juniperus scopulorum* 'Skyrocket' (H 4 m/13 ft) whose shape is tall and thin, and the rapid, ground-covering *J. horizontalis* (30 cm/12 in), both of which will grow well in an open, well-drained site.

Flights of fancy

*O*rnamental features in gardens have their origins in practicality. Plants grown in rows for food production evolved, over the ages, into pleasure gardens with systems that expanded to parterres and stately terraces or gave way to vast sweeps of planted landscape. Streams or underground springs, used originally as functional water sources for irrigating plants, were converted first to primitive cisterns and ultimately to elaborate waterworks, depending on clever hydraulics to create huge fountains. The fortifications that surrounded the castles of the Middle Ages are not so very far removed from walled gardens – both trap the sun and keep the wind out, and both therefore make growing easier and the garden more beautiful.

Garden ornament also played a vital role in the gardens of earlier times because there were far fewer plants to choose from and therefore the emphasis was naturally placed on layout and permanent features such as walks, alleys, pergolas, and of course fountains, urns and statues. Past garden architects placed great importance on the careful selection and positioning of such structures so that all the parts formed a harmonious whole. The *style* of ornament was dictated by passing fashions, but certain basic rules did emerge, particularly the importance of scale – the effect was considered most pleasing if the ornament was in proportion to the overall size of the garden. In former times, ornaments, particularly garden furniture, were often made of local materials, which perfectly complemented their surroundings, and the same holds true today.

Water

The need to control water in order to ensure a steady supply has been of paramount importance in the successful cultivation of food crops throughout the history of gardening, and all over the world ingenious and sometimes extraordinarily elaborate forms of irrigation have been devised to this end. At the same time successive generations of gardeners have valued water for its intrinsic beauty, revelling in the reflective serenity of lakes and ponds, or the sparkling sound and movement of fountains, cascades and waterfalls.

The Romans devised novel ways of diverting and channelling water into everything from

A formal theme at the Charlottenhof gardens in Germany, including a fine symmetrical pond furnished with plants in containers – such basic elements could be adopted on a smaller scale in a private garden.

Above: these elaborate waterworks and rills at Kleve, Germany, combine formal outline with naturalistic planting.

Below: despite its fanciful form, this water sculpture at the Villa Ile de France blends in well with the natural rock formation; such understated use is particularly effective in the informal garden.

simple rectangular basins to huge stepped fountains such as those excavated at Hadrian's villa at Tivoli. The Arabs too were inspired manipulators of water, for it was one of their most precious natural resources. The Moorish villas at Granada are celebrated for their water features, which include the lotus-shaped basin and the marble or tiled water rill.

Sometimes water features were both functional and ornamental. The Egyptian tomb paintings of Thebes from around 1400 BC depict pools stocked with fish and waterfowl; again, in medieval monastic communities, stew ponds were used for growing carp and other fish to eat on Fridays when meat was forbidden, yet surviving monastic records reveal that the monks also considered these to be features of beauty and places of peace and tranquillity. Later, in the grand gardens of Europe in the sixteenth and seventeenth centuries, water played a hugely important role.

With today's sharpened awareness of environmental issues, modern gardeners see water as having a further attribute, in addition to those recognized by the ancients – that of providing a wildlife habitat. Amphibians such

as frogs and newts, themselves predators of many garden pests, will breed readily in a garden pond, which will also provide drinking water for birds and small mammals. In the first days of spring, bees, dry after the winter dormancy, are often seen drinking at the water's edge, and later in summer, the sight of a drab and grotesque dragonfly larva, crawling up a reed and then splitting open to release an adult which glistens like new enamel, is one that makes all the effort of installing a pond well worthwhile.

WATERFALLS AND FOUNTAINS

Waterfalls and fountains, which until this century depended on natural hydraulics, are made feasible for most of us thanks to the electric submersible pump. Water can be devised to spurt as either single or multi-jets, from the centre of a pond or from a fountain standing in its centre. An isolated fountain, on the other hand, could be used to provide a focal point for the garden.

Something simpler altogether would be a lead cistern with water dribbling in from a supply pipe or circulating pump and flowing over. This would not be difficult to organize and could combine ornament with use by providing a sink in which to dip watering cans or even plunge thirsty pots.

For a more rustic effect, nineteenth-century gardeners loved quiet shady corners, piled with tufa (porous limestone), which oozed water attractively and encouraged mosses and ferns to grow over its surface.

PONDS AND POOLS

Over the centuries, ponds and pools have come in all shapes and sizes, including circular, hexagonal, round-ended, octagonal, rectangular with curved bays such as those popular in the Renaissance, or the long raised canals of the Moors. The classic is a simple hole dug out of the ground to below the water table to form an informal pond surrounded by turf or grass. The eighteenth century excelled in creating massive lakes that provided the perfect foil for their carefully landscaped surroundings, their banks planted with graceful willows, but even a small pond can be used to reflect the landscape around it, with perhaps dwarf maples leaning over the edge instead of giant willows. Such water features were always sympathetically placed in relation to the lie of the land, and even a small pond should be located where it might naturally occur, that is, at the lowest level of the land.

Water has always been used in garden design to provide an extra dimension. The beauty of these Asiatic primulas is doubled by being reflected in the clear surface of the pond.

In small, restricted spaces, it is often simpler and more effective to set up a water feature above ground. In the early 1900s, when raised pools were especially popular, frost caused frequent leakage problems by cracking the rendering used to line the structure. Nowadays, raised pools made of brick and stone can be lined with heavy-duty butyl liners, which, because they are pliable and elastic, can take the rapid expansion and contraction of the ice. When properly laid, with all the wrinkles smoothed out, they are also difficult to see underwater. The edge of the liner can then be hidden by covering it with either a mixture of soil and pebbles, turf or stone. A raised pond must also be pressure-proof; a large volume of water is very heavy.

The designs for water features by Edwin Lutyens and Gertrude Jekyll suit the formal urban garden particularly well, especially where every square metre of space counts. One of their most distinctive water features was the narrow, straight-sided channel known as a rill, a direct descendant of the channels found in the Moorish gardens of Spain, which Jekyll visited in her youth. She used rills to provide strict line and form to their gardens. Once laid down, the harshness of these lines was softened by growing water plants within the rills.

Where the number of shapes employed in the modern garden pool is fairly limited, the best way to get the most out of the overall design is to concentrate on the features that surround it. For inspiration we need look no further than the eighteenth century, which abounded in raised tanks and pools made of lead and decorated on the outside with bas-relief garlands or dolphins, or with formal patterns. The genuine articles are rare and costly nowadays, but several firms manufacture replicas which, although by no means cheap, do enable modern gardeners to enjoy the same decorative effect.

Boundaries, walls and fences

At one time, walls and fences were used purely for defence against marauders and wild animals. In troubled times, they became fortifications with moats and lofty walls. Later, in more tranquil eras, they were transformed into charming garden features.

Barriers were also important for keeping the weather out, reducing wind speed and creating sheltered accommodation for the gardens they enclosed. Internal boundaries enabled separate areas to be closed off, allowing for changes of mood and style within the garden, setting quiet places apart from the more open areas, creating microclimates for shade plants and contriving sun traps for exotic species from warmer parts of the world.

HEDGES

Hedges have traditionally been used as barriers, as a means of delineating specific areas of the garden, and as highly decorative devices in topiary (see page 99), knots (see page 60) and parterres (see page 99). In medieval times, for example, thorny bushes such as bramble or blackthorn proved an effective deterrent against animals and are equally effective today against other unwanted intruders.

On the decorative side, the Romans used finely clipped hedges of yew or box to define walks and terraces and this tradition has passed almost unchanged through the Renaissance to the present day. As well as yew and box, traditionally hedges have also been planted using herbs such as rosemary and lavender, evergreens such as holly, privet and bay, and the deciduous hawthorn and hornbeam.

Where wind is a problem, hedges are in fact more effective than walls, as the foliage will act as a filter through which the wind can pass, considerably reducing its strength. A garden surrounded by walls, on the other hand, will

'trap' the wind so that it is forced to gust back on itself, disturbing any still, warm air that has collected during the day and causing havoc to tender plants.

WALLS

Walls provide not only privacy, but also act as a suntrap, soaking up the heat during the day and slowly releasing it during the night into the soil in the immediate area. Northern European gardeners in the seventeenth century discovered that the new tender plants such as nectarines and peaches that had started to arrive from warmer parts of the world would continue to thrive if they were planted against a south-facing wall and given extra protection during the winter. The simple discovery that a wall backing the kitchen area retained even more heat led to experiments with artificial means of heating. These were often hit and miss. In the 1750s the horticulturist Stephen Switzer came to the assistance of the Duke of Rutland who was, he discovered, heating the boughs but not the roots of his tender fruit trees, which of course need a warm soil if they are to thrive.

A walled garden with its sheltered environment is ideal for growing fruit, vegetables or simply flowers to pick for the house.

Apart from providing the ideal site for growing and training exotic fruit trees, walls also provide an excellent support for a wide range of climbers. Roses fare especially well on walls – except in sunny positions in hot climates where mildew is a problem.

The shaded side of walls can support clematis, ferns, and hydrangeas, which prefer cooler conditions.

The high-walled garden has held a special place throughout the history of gardening as a sanctuary for both people and plants, but the cost of building one is prohibitive for most people these days. A low wall built of brick or stone used as a form of seating or perhaps to surround a patio area is more feasible, and will also act as a suntrap; dry-stone planting is an added attraction. Alternatively, or in addition, walls can be decorated with permanent features, such as wall fountains, plaque stones, sundials and wall pots.

FENCES

In medieval times wattle panels woven out of willow wands provided cheap, effective screening, later to be replaced by the simple wooden palings found around the cottage gardens of Britain. North America has a long tradition of decorative picket fencing, dating back to colonial times. Even early palings had turned tops, simple shapes such as arrow heads or ovals, and were often painted – white was always popular, but bright colours were also used.

One of the most attractive screening materials which is both inexpensive and easy to erect, is trelliswork or *treillage*. This consists of crossing laths of timber, which is then strengthened by timber frames. Trelliswork reached the height of its development in the late eighteenth century, when whole edifices – gazebos, arches, covered bower seats – were constructed largely of trelliswork. With cunning use of lines and angles, it was also used to construct *trompes l'oeils*, giving the illusion of extra space and of dimensions that did not exist. Whether painted or left natural, the effect of trelliswork is of a barrier which is partially translucent, creating a gentle, almost ephemeral effect.

From the climbing plants' point of view, few supports are more ideal than trellis, which provides ample foothold without restricting too much light and air. A trellis screen furnished with a collection of climbing roses is a glorious sight in high summer.

Sadly, wooden laths, however well cared for, are not long lasting, and there are few remaining examples of eighteenth-century trelliswork around today, but the patterns are easy to find and construction, in the hands of a capable carpenter, is simple. An arch or a screen

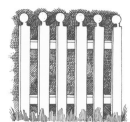

An early American design for a wooden fence.

A simple picket fence surrounds this old-style colonial garden in North America; in earlier times, fences were put up to keep out wandering animals, but such neat boundaries have their own virtues in the small formal garden.

painted white or sage green and installed at the back of a mixed border, for example, will introduce an instant touch of Georgian elegance as well as providing support for a screen of climbers.

Paths, steps and terraces

In early gardens, paths, steps and terraces were strictly functional – in the East, for example, terraces were created to increase the amount of productive land available in hilly and mountainous areas – but these later evolved into highly ornamental features.

PATHS

Paths are used to divide up and link areas of the garden and to provide easy access. In the formal or functional garden, paths are straight, but in the informal garden winding paths can introduce a note of mystery, as long as the final destination is hidden from view. The Japanese excelled in the use of such winding paths in their 'stroll gardens' of the seventeenth century, which took the visitor through a series of carefully designed landscapes. In the same way, the magnificently orchestrated gardens of the seventeenth and eighteenth centuries in Europe used paths to dictate where the walker should admire specific garden compositions and vistas, and even today the careful placing and routing of a path can make a great deal of difference to the appreciation and enjoyment of even the smallest garden.

The simplest paths have always been made of earth or grass, but stones, gravel, brick, flint pebbles or cobblestones present more enduring surfaces and can be laid out to form a variety of decorative patterns. Paving can be of modern slabs, but it looks more mellow, venerable even, if it is constructed from old materials, preferably natural stone. If the stone pieces are broken, they can still be laid, as they might

have been a century ago, as crazy paving or, as the strict Miss Jekyll would have called it, 'random jointing'.

Paths are often bordered in some way, and this is essential for gravel paths, otherwise over time gravel will spill over into the borders. Edgings made of stone or brick are best here. Traditional planted borders include a hedge of shin-high, clipped box; lavender and other sweet-smelling herbs have also been popular.

Above: nothing sets off a flower border so well as an old stone pathway. The strong colours of the flowers here contrast with the greyness of the stone and the plants have draped themselves elegantly on to the paved surface.

Left: there are any number of traditional brick patterns to choose from for laying garden paths. From top to bottom: Spanish bond, running bond, and diagonal herringbone bond.

Above: rock and gravel have been used for the last century and a half as a means of enhancing the plantings of small herbaceous plants. Note the old-fashioned lace pinks growing here.

Right: statuary can be more effective partially obscured by foliage than standing isolated on a plinth.

STEPS AND TERRACES

In the productive garden, steps and terraces were introduced to provide a series of slightly different climates to cater for the widest possible range of vegetables and fruits, for early gardeners had observed that the higher the ground, the more it held the sun's heat. Ornamental garden architects took advantage of this natural phenomenon to site tender plants, often planted in containers, on upper terraces and open verandahs. However, the key function of steps and terraces in the pleasure garden was to introduce different levels and views, which past designers of the great gardens have used to great effect. Today, most of us have to work on a much smaller scale, but even a small series of steps in a naturally sloping garden is attractive, and there are a wide range of materials to choose from in their construction, including treated timber, stones or bricks.

Garden ornaments

Among the ornamental features used in gardens over the centuries, containers such as terracotta pots have proved invaluable in the garden, both as pots for flowers and as inexpensive decorative items which come in a wide range of shapes and sizes, including vases, urns and jars. Garden designers of the Renaissance liked to grow rows of miniature trees in terracotta pots, and this can look very effective today in even a small garden, perhaps lined up to mark the end of a patio or small terrace – or, more simply, with a pot placed either side of the start of a garden path.

Other container shapes to choose from include cisterns, troughs and tubs, much loved by the Romans and enthusiastically taken up in the Renaissance and by garden designers ever since. They were originally used to hold water, but they are also ideal for planting and very

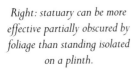

Modern concrete urns, in the author's garden, have developed a 'patina' of maturity over the years and blend with the planting. Single species, like these Verbena 'Sissinghurst', often make a bigger impact than mixed plantings.

Stone trough

Balustrade vase

Terracotta pots

This treillage obelisk brings style to an ornamental kitchen garden and could be used for flowering plants or, as here, climbing beans.

useful where space is limited or where much of the garden is paved over.

Statues have always been popular in the garden – Roman gardens were littered with them – but they are an expensive item, although it is now possible to purchase models made from resin or various reconstituted materials, which are much cheaper than bronze or stone. How you place the statue depends on what style of garden you have. Past garden architects were careful to integrate statues into formal schemes, placing them at the end of paths or vistas, or in the centres of pools, to provide focal points. A device from the past that would work well in a small garden with a hedge is to clip out a niche and place the statue there; the foliage provides an excellent backdrop, and makes the best use of limited space.

In an informal garden, a statue can be placed wherever it will create the right impact – peeping out from a partial covering of foliage perhaps. It might be wise, however, to site it away from the garden's main entrance!

Geometrical forms, such as stone obelisks and pyramids, are particularly well suited to the formal garden where a vertical feature or striking but simple focal point is needed. They were common of course in Ancient Egypt, and the Romans in turn introduced these forms into Western gardens. *Treillage* variations became popular in the seventeenth century, and can be used as a frame for climbing plants. They are particularly useful in the ornamental kitchen garden, where they can be used for growing runner beans or any of the other climbing foods.

Topiary

The simplest form of topiary is the low-clipped hedge, and this was used to considerable effect in the fifteenth century in the form of knot gardens (see page 60). By the eighteenth century

A niche cut in a hedge draws attention to a fine classical statue without sacrificing space. This device would also work well in a small garden.

the knot had evolved into the parterre, and particularly the *parterre de broderie*, the best of which were designed by such architects as London and Wise in England and André Le Nôtre in France. Le Nôtre's influence is apparent in Germany too, which boast some of the finest Baroque parterres still in existence, including those at Herren Hausen.

The complex curvilinear pattern of the *parterre de broderie* was described in dwarf box, and either infilled with coloured earth or with the growing number of interesting plants being introduced by early plant hunters. Such vast, complicated layouts would hardly be applicable

This elaborate parterre at Herren Hausen in Germany is embellished, during summer months, with clipped evergreens – in this case orange trees – in pots. A parterre is too labour-intensive for most gardeners today, but simply trimmed trees or shrubs grown in tubs could be used in pairs to mark the entrance to a small garden or the start of a path; a single form would make an eye-catching focal point anywhere.

Bay makes a fine topiary plant; it is grown here in Versailles tubs and lends a note of formality to this German garden.

To grow young hedging plants to specific shapes, frames made of wood and wire mesh act like moulds, providing the perfect outline to cut to. The beauty of this system is that you need no special hedge-cutting skill to get the shape right. 1. Place the mould over the young tree. 2. As the plant grows through, trim to shape. 3. After a couple of seasons the frame or mould disappears and will eventually rot away.

to modern garden design, but small knot gardens and simplified parterres are very much part of the twentieth-century garden designer's repertoire.

Tree and hedge pleaching is another simple form of training that was common in the past. Trees were used to form screens, by twining and even grafting their lateral branches together, while hedgings such as hornbeam were twined and pruned to form tunnels. These make striking features in a larger garden.

Shaping hedging into geometric forms and figures, the *ars topiari* so popular with the Romans, remained in vogue until the eighteenth century when the Romantic movement swept away such contrived features. Topiary came back into fashion in the nineteenth century and has had its enthusiasts ever since.

The easiest traditional topiary designs to style and maintain are geometric ones such as the pyramid or sphere; more complicated forms such as the closed spiral, cake stand and capped spire all require more trimming.

The most popular plants for topiary work are yew and box, although they are slow growing, and the Italian cypress in milder climates. Other species that lend themselves to simple topiary forms include holly, *Cupressus macrocarpa*, *Viburnum tinus* and bay.

Pruning shears, 1853

Traditional topiary forms include, from left to right, cap or dome, ball and cylinder, spiral, capped dome, and curved pyramid.

Pergolas

Climbing frames of one sort or another have been used for plants in gardens for centuries. The simplest support consists of a series of upright posts set into the ground in pairs and connected by poles across the top.

The more sophisticated pergola became a particular craze in Edwardian days. Sir Lawrence Weaver and Gertrude Jekyll, in *Gardens for Small Country Houses* (1912), mention how widely pergolas were used in Italy, where shade is more in demand than in the colder parts of Europe. Most Italian pergolas consisted of stone or plastered rubble uprights connected by wooden beams. In later years it became fashionable to build the pillars of brickwork, and to top these with cross members of natural wood. Oak or elm were considered ideal because of their hardness and lasting qualities. Nowadays, pergolas are useful for adding height, that most sought-after ingredient, especially in a brand new garden where young plants have yet to achieve stature. As well as supporting elegant flowering climbers, pergolas can be used in the kitchen garden for climbing food plants. Such materials as seasoned oak are expensive but, provided they have been treated with preservatives, many softwoods can be used as cheaper alternatives and can also be easier to cut into elegant shapes.

A pergola can of itself be an attractive garden structure, but is always more effective as a support for climbing plants, even if ultimately they obscure its basic form.

*Nineteenth-century rustic
summerhouse.*

Gazebos, temples and grottos

These could hardly be called functional, unless they doubled as storage accommodation, but they do make delightful features. In *Gardens for Small Country Houses*, commentating on more gracious days, a building big enough to accommodate a small family of modest means is captioned 'A seemly tool-house'. Seemly it may be, but its clapboarding sides, hipped and tiled roof and elegant windows proclaim its high price. Other outbuildings, from Doric temples in the Arcadian landscapes of the eighteenth century to the follies and lodges of the nineteenth century, tended to be decorative but expensive status symbols. But decorative buildings did have their place and they still do in modern gardens, albeit on a humbler scale, by providing focal points, adding interesting contours or just giving somewhere for a path or a vista to lead to.

Vast sums of money can easily be spent on

such luxuries, but more modestly priced out-buildings are also available, particularly those constructed from prefabricated sections. In most gardens these days such buildings will be expected to combine beauty with several functions, but it is perfectly feasible to mimic such old-fashioned follies as temples or even simulated ruins using modern materials. There are firms which specialize in old-looking stonework and others which make classical columns and domes out of such seemingly incongruous high-tech products as fibreglass, plastic or light aluminium alloy!

Furniture

After layout and planting in an ornamental garden, one of the most important design considerations is furniture. Apart from providing the means to socialize, take a meal *al fresco*, or simply recline and enjoy a little peace, furniture helps to underline the style and mood of the garden. The Romans had their stone recliners and there were turf seats in fourteenth-century gardens, but these lack portability and must have been rather damp and chilly on the behind! For the development of the most comfortable furniture on which to sit, relax and enjoy the ambience, we need not look so far back. The nineteenth and early twentieth centuries produced some glorious examples of tables, chairs and benches that were comfortable, elegant and, above all, weather-proof.

Europe's obsession with China in the eighteenth century introduced a taste for *Chinoiserie* to both interior and exterior decoration. Indian-style furniture also crept into Western gardens a century or so ago with the expansion

In a small modern garden, there is not likely to be room for a large grotto or temple, but a period feature like this fountain in the Eremitage gardens, Germany, picked out in coloured stonework to look almost like a mosaic, could on a smaller scale be accommodated almost anywhere.

Below: since Roman times, dovecotes have often been used as garden features. In large gardens, these are sometimes substantial buildings, but this shingled half-barrel design would be at home even in a fairly modest setting.

of the British Empire and has stayed with us to this day, being manifested in the form of seats and benches which are highly decorative but also movable. Earlier styles were adapted by such world-famous architects as Edwin Lutyens, whose oft-imitated Japanese-style benches can still be seen at Sissinghurst castle in England, and today many antique designs are being used in furniture constructed from durable hardwoods.

The industrial revolution and subsequent advance in metal technology spread to outdoor furniture, enabling nineteenth-century gardeners to acquire seats and tables in cast iron, usually with moulded patterns in a rustic style depicting fern leaves or simulated twigs. Traditional blacksmithery at this time was in the process of being overtaken by factory production of wrought iron seats, made from strips of iron or mild steel held together with rivets. Many of these were of complicated design but, being made of thinner metal than the cast

products, were lighter and could therefore be moved about more easily. Some of them even came on their own wheels so that they could be transported to a favourite resting spot. Such designs harmonize perfectly into both period and modern gardens.

The sundial is almost as old as the formal garden. Set here as a centrepiece among informal planting, with a rose arch and statue in the background, the turn of the century is evoked.

'Sundials,' wrote Gertrude Jekyll, 'like other ornaments, depend more for their decorative success on their right placing than on their intrinsic merit as garden sculpture.' The same goes for furniture. A well-crafted, attractive seat placed at the end of a vista or a sundial positioned at the centre of a formal rose garden, even though they may not themselves be hugely important, can become the objects that allow the eye a place to rest once it has taken in all the surrounding scenery of flowers and plants.

The conservatory

Conserving plants under glass has played an increasingly important part in gardening in cold climates during the last couple of centuries. Greenhouses, equipped with heating systems, were developed in the seventeenth century for the specific function of keeping such tender evergreens as oranges and myrtles alive during

the northern winters. Interest in tender plants grew apace so that by the middle of the nineteenth century the passion for collecting exotic plants was reaching a climax.

The biggest difficulty facing the gardeners was in erecting glasshouses that were big enough and *light* enough to allow tender exotic plants to develop. Creating large rooms was easy enough, but wide areas of unsupported roof needed so much structure that it was difficult to glaze them. The solution to the problem was found in 1816 by the redoubtable J. C. Loudon, who invented a lightweight, iron glazing bar. This was strong enough to support a structure of glass but thin enough to let in maximum daylight. Loudon's idea was soon copied and by the middle of the nineteenth century, glass buildings capable of accommodating large exotic collections were springing up everywhere. The Victorians turned their conservatories into leisure areas complete with elegant furniture made out of wickerwork and cast iron.

As the middle classes grew in numbers, demand for smaller conservatories and plantaria attached to the house increased. Loudon, a shining example of the self-made man, built himself a tiny domed glasshouse at the front of his house in Porchester Terrace, London. In it he grew, among other plants, tender camellias and florists' hyacinths. The fashion for domes, porticoes and other fancy structures on small-scale conservatories grew with the rising tide of exotics available for general cultivation. Utilitarian greenhouses also grew in numbers until no self-respecting villa dweller was without the means of raising and nurturing his or her own tender plants, from exotic scarlet pelargoniums similar to the ones Queen Victoria demanded for her own gardens at Buckingham Palace to the subtropical ferns seen in the front windows of every genteel suburban terraced house.

Today's revival of the conservatory craze

recent years have seen the regrowth of the conservatory industry and the development of an even wider range of 'Victorian' glasshouses than the real Victorians were ever able to enjoy.

In their revival, however, some of the special advantages of nineteenth-century conservatories have been lost. The most important of these is ventilation. The classic Victorian conservatory was a large building with a high, often turretted, roof and was therefore much more airy and better ventilated compared to the scaled-down versions that are available today. Moreover, Victorian conservatories frequently had a greater number of roof vents and side windows. When selecting a traditional style conservatory, therefore, it is important that, as well as having period looks, the building works at least as efficiently as an old one would have done. What reproduction buildings lack in windows that will open – each one of which adds to the cost – can be compensated for these days by electric extraction fans. (When it comes to conserving heat in winter, however, it has to be said that modern materials and double glazing techniques insulate far more effectively than the original single glass and steel glazing bar constructions.)

A great many design features of earlier periods are so attractive that they are worth imitating in our gardens purely for their own appearance. But many of these features evolved as solutions to specific design problems, and as such are as relevant to gardens today as to those of yesteryear. The *trompe l'oeil*, for example, is a cunning device to minimize that perennial problem of properties in the 1990s – limited space. And planting to create a narrow vista and placing an object as a focal point at its end, though an ancient concept, is a useful way of transforming an awkward corridor into a delightful walk.

Nineteenth-century horticulturists, as well as being avid collectors of new plants, liked to display their exotica in large conservatories, many of which became extensive indoor gardens. A similarly fine display can be reproduced in a more modest greenhouse.

comes after a long decline in their use. Heating costs proved to be the biggest disincentive, and maintenance of such buildings was costly. Loudon's iron glazing bars may have been light and strong, but they were also quick to corrode in the hot, humid atmosphere of the conservatory. With modern technology giving us a much better understanding of insulation, and with more corrosion-resistant materials available,

THE
WORKING
GARDEN

The most traditional methods of gardening have evolved from centuries of tried-and-tested practical experience, and the old-fashioned ways of tending the soil, fertilizing, propagating and pest control are often simply the most effective for the job. Modern reliance on artificial aids may allow instant control of pests, fast cultivation and even the growing of plants in otherwise totally unsuitable conditions, but we are now aware of the environmental damage such short-term solutions can cause, and how much more satisfying and challenging it is to garden the natural way.

Tools and equipment

*I*t is hardly surprising, when you consider that tilling the soil by hand is much the same activity today as it was in prehistoric times, that many of the tools of early mankind are still with us, essentially unchanged. The simpler the job, the simpler the tool, and such basic actions as scratching or turning over the soil, breaking up clods or digging trenches for drainage have been accomplished with hoes, mattocks and spades for time immemorial.

Sophistication in horticulture has brought its own tools, of course, whether they be devices for shaving lawns, gadgets for perfecting

Old-fashioned gardeners were less inclined to throw old or broken tools away than we are today. Here, a collection of tools, including border forks, awaits new handles.

topiary or special grafting knives. Some, like cucumber-straightening glasses, have passed in and out of use with changing fashions and become amusing curios. Others, such as hand-operated multiple shears or horse-drawn lawn mowers, have been replaced by modern machinery, but their functions are as applicable to gardening in the 1990s as they were at the time of their invention. Indeed, I can remember, back in the 1970s, watching grass areas in New Delhi being cut with antique lawn mowers drawn by oxen!

With the current re-evaluation of modern horticultural techniques and the move towards more organic, or at least more environmentally friendly, gardening, it would serve us well to look at both the range of tools any gardener needs and those tools from previous eras that might be put to good use today in the organic garden. In fact, the essentially unchanging nature of most tools indicates that most old-fashioned tools are ultimately the best designed for the job.

Breaking the ground

Making the transition from grazing to cropping was an early step towards civilization. It is as well to remember, perhaps with irony, that Abel was a herdsman, while Cain was the first tiller of the soil, and also the first man to display a deadly neurosis. Might it have been better for mankind – and the planet – if we had all remained as nomads, footloose and fancy free? As it was, God responded to Cain's fratricide by giving him horribly infertile land with which to endeavour to grow his crops. It's been an uphill struggle ever since!

The earliest tools were probably primitive axes used to chop the earth. Remains of hoe-like tools have been discovered in the Tigris and Euphrates delta in Southwest Asia, their blades made of stone fixed to wooden handles with bitumen gathered from natural sources in the area. Although the materials used in the manufacture of such implements have changed, first with the use of iron and associated blacksmithery, and later with such materials as stainless steel and plastic, the basic design of the adze-shaped hoe or mattock has remained much the same throughout the millennia. The mode of operation is simple: a downward blow drives the blade into the ground; lifting the handle breaks off the sod; dragging the handle towards you disturbs the earth and turns some of it over. Repeated light downward blows chop large clods into smaller pieces, eventually preparing a tilth, so that with the handle held vertically, the flat blade can then be used to firm the broken soil down. Thus, the mattock can be used for almost every operation from breaking new ground to preparing a seed bed. It is the ultimate garden tool, though in its unrefined state, one that must have been cumbersome and tiring to use.

THE SPADE

The spade is probably used more than any other tool in the garden, and today's stainless-steel models make digging as easy as possible. Spades were used in Roman times and, though less ancient than the mattock, have been a feature of all gardening for thousands of years. One of the fourteenth-century seats at Lincoln cathedral in England has a carving of a robed gardener wielding a wooden spade. The blade has been clad in iron, but it is unlikely that the tool would have been strong enough to handle

virgin earth and it would have been heavy to use for long periods, even for a toughened medieval gardener.

The main improvement to the spade was first the development of the iron blade, followed by the steel blade. Fixed to a wooden haft with rivets, the iron spade was lighter and more resilient than earlier, iron-shod models. The metal could be ground to a sharp edge, making it more efficient at cutting into the sod. Of the various styles and shapes that have evolved since then, the most common today are steel spades and shovels with short handles and squared-off blades – favoured in much of Britain – and long-handled versions with curved blades that taper to a point, as seen in much of North America and in France. The mode of action is similar for both, but users of each invariably swear that theirs is best and

A well-ordered tool shed is an essential prerequisite of the efficient kitchen gardener.

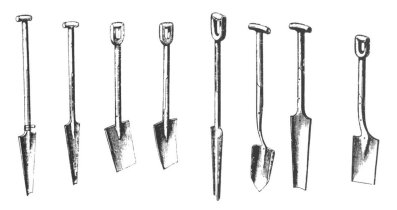

Garden spades

66 *If* A GARDENER WERE LIMITED TO THE
CHOICE OF ONLY ONE IMPLEMENT, THAT WHICH
HE WOULD RETAIN AS THE MOST USEFUL,
WOULD BE THE SPADE. 99

The Gardener's Assistant, 1859

that the other is less efficient. In the nineteenth century particularly, a range of specialist designs was developed, with narrow-bladed models for digging out drains – or rabbits – and even cut-away blades specifically designed to add lightness to heavy soils.

In the Middle Ages the more favoured tool was the breast spade or breast plough. This was essential for the technique known as 'slash and burn', where the surface of an area to be cultivated was skimmed of weeds and turf, together with the top inch or so of soil. This was allowed to dry and then burnt, the resulting ashes being spread back on the land. The breast plough had a carved, flat blade, a long haft and a strengthened cross piece which, in

use, would fit snugly into the groin or against the thighs of the operator who could then put his whole weight behind the plough, sliding the blade through the turf.

This implement came in dozens of variations. The seventeenth-century writer, Gervais Markham, illustrates a turf-cutting spade with a pointed blade, shaped like an arrow, and in his *Encyclopaedia of Gardening* (1822), John Claudius Loudon describes others. Loudon pointed out just how heavy and cumbersome most of these archaic tools were: '. . . they are adapted for labour which requires more force than skill,' he wrote. 'They are generally large and require the use of both hands and the muscular action of the whole frame.'

Breast ploughs ceased to be used at the end of the nineteenth century, superseded by a change in techniques rather than improved tools. However, they would still be useful implements for lifting turf, especially used in conjunction with a second, sharp-sided tool for slicing the turfs.

Every gardener needs at least one good spade, and the best are made from stainless steel. You'll find most modern spades now have plastic handles, but wooden ones are preferable. They're more comfortable to use and they look nicer.

Below: a seventeenth-century engraving showing gardeners at work preparing the ground for an orchard.

This collection of old-fashioned tools includes rakes for cultivating a fine tilth and multi-headed clippers for neat hedge work.

Parkes' steel digging forks,
1859

Tilling and cultivating

Once the turf was lifted, lighter tools such as hoes, rakes and forks could come into play.

Forks The garden fork evolved from a pronged object, known nowadays in some agricultural parts of England as a spud, which is designed to remove individual, deep-rooted weeds such as docks or thistles. Early garden forks were three-tined and were forged with rounded, sharp tines for cultivation purposes or with flat, duller tines to facilitate the harvesting of such root crops as potatoes. The best modern forks are made of forged steel fitted with a wooden or metal handle (avoid the cheaper pressed-steel forks, which easily buckle when pressure is applied).

Rakes Soil must be raked level before it can be sown, and illustrations of sixteenth- and seventeenth-century rakes show that those

used for cultivation consisted of rows of flattened, delta-shaped blades which scored the earth, helping to create the desired tilth. Nowadays, we have forged-steel rakes which are easy to handle. Rakes designed for gathering grass or hay were, and still are, made of timber for lightness, but were once wider and longer in the tooth (*see also* page 123).

Hoes The heavier mattocks used to break up the soil eventually evolved into lightweight hoes for ruffling the surface to dislodge weed seedlings, or into claw-like drags for breaking clods down into a fine tilth, ready for seed sowing. Over the centuries, various regional differences in these tools have developed. The

Tools such as hoes have changed but little over the centuries.
Those on the right, near the two-pronged pitchfork, are
examples of the Dutch or push-hoe.

swan-necked hoe, or draw hoe, for example, which is pulled through the soil, is replaced in some areas by the Dutch hoe, or push hoe, which is pushed forward in action – an easier job in the rich, friable loams of Holland than on heavy or stony soil, where the hacking movements of the swan-necked hoe are more likely to achieve the desired results. Both are also useful weeding implements in the garden, the Dutch hoe for loosening weed seedlings and the swan-necked hoe for removing well-established weeds.

Trowel The garden trowel has been with us since the 1600s and is the offspring of an extraordinary gadget known as a transplanter. This looked like a primitive hand drill with a bend in the handle for leverage. Instead of a drill bit, it had a channel-shaped business end which could be twisted into the ground round a selected plant, enabling the user to cut and lift the plant in its own plug of soil, and hence transplant it with minimal root disturbance. Trowels continue to be rounded and are still the most useful tools for transplanting small plants and seedlings, particularly in the ornamental garden.

Hand fork Another traditional implement with a long pedigree, the small hand fork is

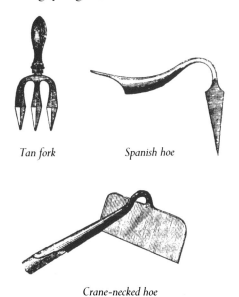

Tan fork   *Spanish hoe*

Crane-necked hoe

particularly useful for weeding borders. *The Gardener's Assistant* (1859) also recommends its use 'in pits and frames'.

Growing containers These date back in fact to ancient Egypt, but the modern terracotta flowerpot, with drainage holes and a tapering side, was widely favoured in the seventeenth century. Francis Gentil, in his *Le Jardinier Solitaire* (1706), illustrates various types of pot and describes their uses thus: 'To put Flowers in, that grow better so than in full earth, such as Pinks, Bear-Ears [*Primula auricula*], Tube-roses [*Polyanthus tuberosa*] etc. These may be either of plain Earth, or of Dutch Ware, the former are much larger for holding Jassamine and Clove Gill Flowers [clove-scented pinks used for flavouring wine].' Clay pots have a number of advantages over plastic ones. Because they are porous, they allow the air to circulate freely and drainage is improved. They are also heavier, which is a bonus when growing top-heavy plants. Conversely, clay pots must be very thoroughly cleaned and sterilized after each use, and you need to water more often so the compost does not dry out.

Top: Traditional terracotta pots look more attractive than modern plastic ones, and tend to drain more efficiently; being porous, they also help to prevent water-logging. However, they can become encrusted with limescale and will need scrubbing before use.

Below: antique rhubarb forcers lined up at the edge of the garden ready for next year.

Watering devices Hand-held watering devices with roses or lots of small holes to create a gentle shower effect for watering young seedlings predate the fifteenth century. Early types were made of earthenware, the whole pot being peppered with holes, and were useful for damping down the rushes on floors in the house. Later models carried spouts, with or without roses. By the seventeenth century, a range of water pots had been devised, including a model with a perforated bottom that enabled the user to apply liquid fertilizers – made by infusing the dung of sheep or poultry in the water – to the soil around plants without splashing any on the foliage, which the solution would burn.

A hose pipe is an invaluable piece of equipment for watering the garden. A form of hose pipe was used in the sixteenth century. Thomas Hill, in *The Gardener's Labyrinth* (1652), describes a large copper watering pot to which is attached a 'long pipe ful of little holes on the head'. By the middle of the nineteenth century hose pipes were made of leather with studded seams or, less expensive but also less durable, of calico which had been waterproofed with a mixture of linseed oil and soap. There were frequent technical problems with these primitive materials, however, and the use of hoses did not become general until the introduction in 1845 of the Red Rubber Garden and Yard Hose by the Gutta Percha Company.

Nowadays, hoses are made of hardwearing plastic, and the best kind are those that are stored on a through-feed reel so that the

amount of hose unrolled can be easily controlled. A seep hose is also useful in some gardens. The pipe has evenly spaced holes along its length to allow water to drip away slowly, and it can be kept more or less permanently in place (water shortages permitting!).

Sprinklers may not seem to be very traditional, but they are a useful addition to any garden, and they have in fact been around, in one form or another, for some time. Again, we learn from Thomas Hill (1652) that a form of sprinkler was used in the sixteenth century

Watering is important to obtain optimum results in the kitchen garden and, where waterlines are not piped in, a useful alternative is the water cart. The tank itself pivots and, for the less strong, the cart can be hitched to a pony.

called a 'great Squirt', a large tub made of tin which incorporated a hand-operated pump mechanism to force the water upwards so that 'in the breaking may fall as drops of raine'. The result was probably more like a downpour! The modern sprinkler produces a fine spray, and the best models have the sprinkler head positioned well above the ground.

Propagating and protecting

Successful propagation is the key to all gardening and although success partly depends on whether or not the person propagating has green fingers, certain garden structures and equipment have been in use for so long that they seem now to be almost indispensable.

GREENHOUSES

Greenhouse design has changed little over the years, although generally speaking the older ones were better ventilated but the best of the modern ones are more efficient at conserving

heat. Comments in *The Gardener's Assistant* (1859) on greenhouses and orangeries of the previous century are somewhat trenchant: 'Formerly they were built with upright glass in front, no light being admitted by the roof, back, or ends, and even much of the frontage was occupied with too massive architecture to permit sufficient light to reach the plants; but such as it was the plants inclined towards it, and their growth was what is termed *one-sided*.' The author goes on, 'The importance of light for vegetation has of late years become better known than formerly, and great improvements have accordingly been made in the construction of greenhouses and conservatories. Instead of dark roofs very light ones are constructed; and plants can now be grown fit to be seen on all sides.'

By the 1850s the basic greenhouse shapes had been established: the lean-to, three-quarter span and full span-roof. The lean-to is built against the sunny side of a wall and has one sloping roof supported by a vertical side. It has the advantage of being able to use heat stored

Greenhouses, popular since the eighteenth century, are important for providing an artificially warm environment, not only for producing fruit and flowers out of season, but also for propagating seedlings, rooting cuttings and over-wintering tender plants.

Above: winter in the greenhouse can be colourful when pot plants such as Cyclamen primula obconia *are grown in large groups.*

in the wall and emitted during the night when the temperature has dropped. The three-quarter span, or north light, is also a lean-to construction but has a small span up from the top of the wall to admit diffused light – a valuable addition for such light-hungry crops as peaches or nectarines. The major disadvantage of the lean-to is the limitation of light. As *The Gardener's Assistant* points out, 'plants may be grown very well, but not so symmetrically as in span-roofed structures, or others that admit light on all sides of the plants.'

The full span greenhouse consists of a roof with two slopes like an inverted V, which 'is very advantageous for the growth of plants that are dwarf and cannot conveniently be placed in a lean-to so near the glass as they ought to be. Another advantage is the admission of light on both sides. Equality of growth is more easily maintained, however more expensive to heat.'

Other variations included the ridge and furrow, vineries, peach houses and even cherry houses. There were even wall frames where areas of warm wall could be covered with a form of lean-to, some of which could be removed in summer.

Lean-tos and span-roofs can either have all-glass sides or can rest on a base wall of brick or stone. The advantage of an all-glass side is that tall crops such as tomatoes or chrysanthemums can be accommodated in full light, and even when staging is introduced, plants can be grown, in reasonable light conditions, beneath it. This is particularly useful for shade-loving plants, and newly stuck cuttings which would wilt in direct sunlight. An all-glass house is more expensive to heat, however, than a greenhouse with a base wall. The latter will also stay cooler in summer, whereas with the all-glass greenhouses the problem is the opposite – keeping it cool in summer.

Traditionally, greenhouses have been constructed out of glass and wood. Nowadays it is more common to find greenhouses consisting of lightweight but strong aluminium frames with either polythene or rigid polycarbonate sheets. With their various engineering features, aluminium houses are quicker and easier to build and have the advantage of being lightweight. They also admit more light because aluminium glazing bars are thinner than wood.

Although more expensive to build, the traditional greenhouse does have certain advantages over the aluminium and plastic greenhouse. The wood frame, for example, does absorb some heat during the day which is then

The traditional full span greenhouse design.

released at night, easing the expense of artificial heating. The glass is also able to trap the sun's warmth, and as a material it will last much longer than the modern polythene, which has to be replaced every couple of years. Rigid plastic sheets scratch quite easily, creating small grooves that capture dirt and reduce transparency, and it may also become brittle and crack from weathering. Softwood frames need regular painting but red cedar contains natural preservatives and stands up to the weather well, although it will benefit from a biennial oiling. Aluminium frames, on the other hand, are maintenance-free. Nevertheless, wooden-frame greenhouses are much more attractive, particularly as part of an ornamental kitchen garden.

A greenhouse is invaluable in the garden for propagating, raising food and prolonging the growing season, and for over-wintering half-hardy perennials. Regardless of what is grown in a greenhouse, good ventilation is essential. There should be at least one ventilator for each 1.5 m (5 ft) of roof span and adequate side ventilation as well. As far as the position of the greenhouse is concerned, most gardeners have favoured either a north–south direction, which means it will receive more light during a full year, but an east–west position ensures maximum light during the winter months. Whichever direction is chosen, shade will be needed in summer; this was supplied traditionally in the form of roller-like blinds or by using washable paint on the glass. All greenhouses contain sets of shelves and staging for all kinds of plants, but traditional greenhouses usually also featured a potting bench for potting and possibly a hotbed – a manure bed to create artificial heat – for forcing early crops. Traditional greenhouses, as well as being productive, were also made to look attractive with flowering pot plants and even tender shrubs in decorative tubs.

Glasshouse production of mixed crops needs expert management. On a smaller scale, it is best to stick to one or two items, or to grow plants with similar growing needs: tomatoes with green peppers and aubergines might be a useful combination.

COLD FRAMES

Cold frames were widely used by Parisian market gardeners from the seventeenth century onwards, and the French were famed for their *culture maraîchère*, or intensive gardening, which also included the widescale use of hotbed frames and plenty of manure. By 1727 Stephen Switzer notes that hotbed frames and what he calls forcing houses were used from mid November to force lettuce, chervil, cresses and mint, and by the nineteenth century cold frames were being used for growing flowers and vegetables and – now their primary use – as nursery areas. Cold frames are designed to be opened and closed, according to the weather, so that young plants can gradually become acclimatized to an outdoor life. For producing early crops, a cold frame is indispensable. Seed of most hardy plants will germinate readily under the protection of the glass but will not overheat or grow too soft.

The important thing to remember when constructing a frame is not to make it too deep – plants should not be farther from the glass than they need be and it is important to make

Monro's cannon greenhouse boiler, 1859

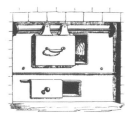

Sylvesters' greenhouse furnace doors, 1859

sure that there is an adequate fall from the back of the frame to the front for rain to run off the roof. Make sure the frame is sited in a sheltered location in the garden, so that the effect of cold winds is minimized.

Plants raised in a greenhouse need to be gradually introduced to outdoor conditions in a process known as hardening off, which is done in the cold frame (putting plants straight into the ground in early spring from a warm greenhouse, for example, would severely affect their growth and, at worst, they will perish). To harden off, place greenhouse seedlings into the cold frame for at least two weeks before they are due to be planted out. Leave the lid closed for the first 48 hours unless the days are extremely hot. On the third day leave the top open slightly to begin acclimatizing the plants, but close it again at night. Gradually increase the opening each day until the lid can be left off altogether during the daytime and with the top very slightly open at night. At this point, the top should slowly be left more and more open at night until it can be removed completely; the plants are then ready to be planted out.

Frames are also useful in winter, in mild areas, for autumn sowing of vegetables such as spinach or indoor lettuces that mature through winter to spring, and for growing early vegetables in spring. Traditionally, frames have also been used to grow melons and cucumbers. Frames should, as a rule, admit as much light as possible in winter and early spring. During summer, however, the glass can be painted with shading paint or a shading material laid over the glass and the frame used to house indoor plants such as cyclamen and primulas.

In autumn, the cold frame can be used as a staging post in reverse, getting plants ready for winter in the greenhouse. Bulbs such as freesias or narcissus can be placed in pots or trays in the frame and brought indoors later for forcing. If valuable space is being taken up in the

greenhouse for growing tomatoes and it is time to bring chrysanthemums in, the chrysanthemums can be stood in their pots in frames until the tomatoes have been cleared away to make room for them. Even long-term sowings of tree seeds, which may take more than a year to germinate, will sit happily in a cold frame – where you can keep an eye on them – and left to spring to life when they are good and ready.

Cloches

Propagation in any but the most gentle of climates is much easier if the plants can be protected. On a small scale, leaving aside such modern boons as windowsill propagators or even the humble plastic bag, it is the cloche that, historically, has provided the cheapest and most effective means of plant protection outside. The cloche covers a small area of ground with a protective but translucent shell, enabling the gardener to create a tiny microclimate within which delicate young plants can thrive. By keeping off winter rain, cloches prevent plants from rotting, while their heat-trapping effect brings forward spring and lengthens the season. These benefits are subsidiary, however, to the chief purpose of the cloche, which is to protect vulnerable plants from frost.

Cloche simply means 'bell' in French and the

Top: the cold frame is used not only to raise fruit and vegetables which need protection, but also as a means of nursing young stock through its tender weeks by giving shelter and, later, by allowing a gradual hardening-off.

Below: modern plastic versions of bell cloches may be lighter to carry, but these glass cloches will not blow away, even in the strongest of gales.

Above: Pilkington's bell glass, 1859

Right: these beautiful Victorian hand lights have removable tops and are as effective as modern plastic cloches and more sturdy.

Below: nineteenth-century Wardian case

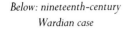

first cloches were no more than bell-shaped jars inverted over the subject plants. Most had a handle at the top for easy manoeuvrability, but not all were made of glass. Gentil (1706) illustrates domes made of straw, looking very much like old-fashioned beehives, which were designed to protect newly planted subjects fresh from the greenhouse against sun scorch or wind damage. By the nineteenth century bell-jars had been replaced by hand lights, which were usually constructed out of cast iron glazing bars and panes of glass, but they were still bottomless, and therefore useless for transporting plants, a serious drawback in an age obsessed with plant collecting. What was needed was a kind of travelling cloche which would ensure the safe transit of plants in their own environment. Nathaniel Bagshaw Ward (1791–1868) provided the answer, with the Wardian case.

Ward was a doctor who lived and practised in London's docklands, but who, as a naturalist, spent much of his spare time out in the countryside. He brought a chrysalis home one

day and, to ensure that it hatched off safely, inverted a large glass jar over the soil in which he had placed his catch. The microclimate he had thus created, as well as ensuring the well-being of the moth-to-be, stimulated a germination of seedlings in the soil, inspiring him to develop a carrying case in which plants could be transported through inhospitable climates in relative safety. The so-called Wardian cases were used by plant hunters for the next century, but they became especially popular in Victorian households as plantaria, especially useful for plants such as ferns, which require a humid environment.

Cutting, disciplining and pruning

Since so much gardening of earlier centuries was formal, and since formality depends on a geometry of straight lines, symmetrical curves and considered angles, there has long been a need for implements which help to enforce garden discipline.

An old-fashioned kitchen garden with trained and clipped box.

Even among early Renaissance horticulturists the use of callipers and rulers was necessary to ensure accurate measurement in garden layout. Just as essential was a garden line wound on to a reel for marking out the designs; the most functional were mounted on long spikes so that they could stand in the ground. And then, once planted, the garden subjects themselves needed to be clipped and pruned to keep them to precise shapes. Sixteenth- and early seventeenth-century evergreens and hedges were trimmed with hooked knives specially designed for the purpose.

Shears The first hand shears were used for shearing sheep, and many an old gardener, to this day, uses them to trim and tidy. Held in one hand, they are sprung so that they pop open and need pressure to close them. They are unwieldy, except in the hands of an experienced sheep shearer, and the single-handed action causes muscle fatigue very quickly. Early two-handed gardening shears illustrated by Gentil (1706) look awkward and impractical, with large handles set wide apart and odd-shaped blades. It is probable that skilled topiarists of the early eighteenth century still preferred to work with their hedging knives. Even today, a skilled hedger, with bill hook and

sickle, can maintain and restore a field hedge to a far higher standard than can any machine, though it may take him a month to do what a flail cutter can slash through in an hour.

Later shears were more thoughtfully designed. J.C. Loudon (1822) describes several, including those designed for verge trimming, edge cutting and even long-handled affairs that were supposed to enable the user to cut hedges that had grown out of reach. Loudon also reported dozens of inventions and gadgets in his *Gardener's Magazine*. Many were, no doubt, useful, but it must be supposed that the majority of those new gadgets, however brilliant in concept, were useless to the practical gardener. *Plus ça change . . !*

Today, most gardeners need only two kinds of shears, a short-handled pair which is ideal for trimming hedges, and a long-handled pair for neatening the edge of the lawn.

Pruners, knives and saws By the end of the nineteenth century, gardeners were able to select from a bewildering range of equipment. Catalogues whose illustrations were reminiscent of a surgeon's collection of instruments listed pruners, trimmers, pocket knives, loppers and saws designed for every aspect of plant discipline. Some of the inventions were fanciful and their advertisements depicted gentlemen, dressed up in smart suits and even top hats, clipping or hosing with one hand while they smoked a cheroot or dandled an infant with the other.

Secateurs and a pair of long-handled pruners for tackling larger shrubs and trees will serve the needs of most gardeners today. If you have large areas of hedge to trim, mechanical hedge cutters, which are light and easy to operate, are a boon. A pruning saw can be handy too for reaching awkward branches, and a budding knife, which is specially designed for the job with a notch cut into the blade, is the best tool for budding.

Parrot-bill shears

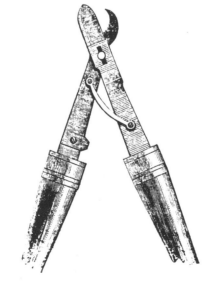

Grass

Surely the most fruitful breeding ground for complicated gadgetry has been grass. In agriculture, the history of mowing and grass conservation, be it silage or hay, makes fascinating reading, but in gardening, where grass is so often the equivalent of the fitted carpet in an interior, more money is spent on its upkeep – grooming, feeding, watering and mollycoddling – than any other part of the property.

The problem with grass is that if it grows, it needs regular mowing but, if it fails to thrive, it can look patchy and ruin the landscape.

Close-mown grass is the most problematical, because it needs the most attention. In the stately gardens of the English landscape era – from around 1730 to the end of the century – sheep were used to crop grass right up to the walls of the house. The alternative was to have the grass close-mown with scythes. To scythe properly, the implements had to be razor-sharp and needed operating by a man of great skill. After the cut, the mown grass was raked up using wooden rakes and carted away. To combat frost action, grass needed rolling too, either with heavy horse- or man-drawn rollers.

The first lawn mower with a cylindrical cutting mechanism was patented in Britain by Edwin Beard Budding in 1830. The principle was based on machinery used in the textile

> **66** *Nothing* REFRESHES THE SIGHT SO MUCH AS FINE SHORT GRASS. **99**
>
> Albertus Magnus, 1260

A metal roller is essential for the lawn enthusiast. It is also useful for laying pathways through the vegetable plot and for helping to break down dried, cloudy soil without compacting the subsoil.

industry to create an even finish on fabrics with a pile. The Suffolk firm of Ransomes were the first large-scale manufacturers of lawn mowers. These first models had to be pushed, but there were extra handles in front for a second man to help pull them through rough or long grass.

Later mowers, patented in both Britain and the United States, could be pulled by small draught animals such as donkeys or ponies, often shod in special soft shoes to prevent divots. In the 1850s in England, Samuelson of Banbury launched a machine which mowed and rolled at the same time and was driven by pony power. By the end of the nineteenth century power mowers, driven by steam and, later, by petrol, gradually replaced horse-drawn models, but these were really only suitable for larger gardens. Mechanized mowers for small lawns did not appear in any appreciable quantity until between the World Wars.

Subsequent developments have superseded the cylinder mower in most small private gardens, but wherever a perfect, level sward is needed by an exacting groundsman, the cylinder mower, based on Budding's design, is still the machine of choice.

For all its perfect cutting, the biggest disadvantage with the cylinder mower is that it is easy to knock out of alignment. Well-tempered and with sharpened blades, it will cut to perfection, but a single misplaced pebble or twig can misalign the blades and spoil the even cut. Modern rotary mowers are far more tolerant of amateur users and models with rear rollers create a striped effect almost as attractive as that achieved with a cylinder machine.

In modern times, although the horticultural trade reels each year with the onslaught of innovative gadgets, few totally revolutionary tools or machines have emerged. Shredders for preparing compost more efficiently have increased in consumption, following the trend to

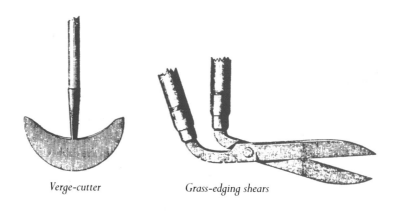

Verge-cutter   *Grass-edging shears*

conserve natural resources more carefully. Trimmers which strip grass and weeds with whirling nylon cords cater for the modern obsession with tidiness, and there are also mechanical hedge cutters which are light and easy to operate.

Among hand tools, hoes and mattocks and spades are still with us. In the 1960s Wilkinson Sword developed an ergonomically designed hoe, known as a 'Swoe', with three cutting edges in stainless steel set at a useful angle into a lightweight alloy handle. The action is simple, reducing fatigue, and the clean blade slides through soil with the greatest of ease, but it is, after all, no more than a simple tool which could as easily have been designed by the Roman poet and gardener Virgil as by the research and development team of a modern steel company.

A restful expanse of finely mown grass in a well-planted American garden.

Grass meadows are seldom close-cut. The kind of equipment used before the advent of tractors and mechanical mowers consisted of a scythe, wooden hay rake and pitch fork. On lawns, the besom broom was used to sweep up any loose grass cuttings.

Propagation

The art of propagation has been an essential skill for gardeners throughout history. For the uninitiated, it may seem like hard work, and with so many well-stocked nurseries and garden centres selling plants all year, it might also appear to be an unnecessary skill to acquire nowadays. But raising your own plants from seed and cuttings is far easier than you might think. It is also inexpensive, once you have equipped yourself with the essential tools to launch what amounts to a pocket industry, and can be the greatest fun. Apart from the satisfaction of growing precisely the plants you want, there is also a deep and lasting pleasure in watching the development of your plant treasures from scratch.

Most people start with fairly unchallenging species and will then want to progress to more difficult plants. That is usually the point at which they find that the great majority of garden plants are simple to raise and that the tricky ones are few and far between!

Besides being a cheap way of acquiring more plants, propagation is worthwhile for a number of other reasons. Quite often, especially with the old-fashioned plants, the variety you seek is either difficult and expensive to buy from a nursery or may only be available from a fellow gardener. It is not easy to ask someone for a whole plant, but perfectly commonplace and undemanding to ask for a pinch of seed or a small cutting.

One of the joys of gardening, particularly with old-fashioned or unusual plants, is that there is a whole network of enthusiasts – not just nationwide but internationally – who are keen to exchange plant material. So if you are giving and receiving seed, you had better know how to raise it! Every plantsman knows the embarrassment of the question, 'How did those seeds do – the ones that I gave you last spring?' and the guilt at remembering that they are still festering in their packet in the potting shed!

Propagation also enables you to ensure against loss, particularly with vulnerable species. If your plants are ageing or are susceptible to winter losses, it is reassuring to know that you have rooted some healthy young specimens to replace them if disaster strikes.

Newly rooted cuttings can be planted out in a frame or protected corner to grow on until ready for transplanting.

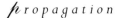

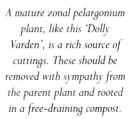

A mature zonal pelargonium plant, like this 'Dolly Varden', is a rich source of cuttings. These should be removed with sympathy from the parent plant and rooted in a free-draining compost.

The way plants grow is timeless, and precisely the same rules apply today as they did a thousand years ago. Some of the propagating methods discussed here, therefore, will not be new to seasoned gardeners. There is nothing modern about grafting, for example, or seed sowing or taking cuttings. Mist and fog propagation, where air is humidified by machine, is only 'new' in that the technology involved has reduced the human input. The only truly space-age propagating method is by tissue culture, where individual cells are grown in a nutrient gel until tiny plantlets are formed. Although widespread, only a minority of commercially raised plants are multiplied in this way, and the majority of nursery stock worldwide is still increased in much the same way as it has been for hundreds of years.

Grafting and budding

Of all the means of multiplying stock, grafting is probably the one most shrouded in mystique. It is an ancient technique, used for example by

Pruning knife, left, and grafting knife, right, 1859

125

the Romans, to graft otherwise slow-growing roses, and by the ancient Chinese in the raising of tree paeonies. It does require considerable skill, however, and is therefore less often attempted by amateur gardeners than other methods, but is nonetheless productive and satisfying to try.

Grafting provides a means of propagating plants that are difficult to multiply in any other way. Domestic varieties of apples, for example, are almost impossible to grow from cuttings and will not come true from seed. They must therefore be grafted on to crab apple rootstocks, which grow far more vigorously. Over the centuries, the quality of such rootstocks has been improved so that today it is possible to buy fruit trees grafted on to different types to provide trees that will carry the same variety of fruit but which will vary in growth rate and habit. Apples and other fruit grafted to dwarf rootstocks are especially useful for small modern gardens where space is restricted, but, since trees give so much more to a garden than merely fruit, the older-style trees, grown to large standards, can also be used to make venerable features. Sadly, few nurseries provide fruit trees grafted to such vigorous stocks these days, so one solution – if rather long term – is to graft your own.

The object of grafting is to bring the vital tissues – found just below the layer of bark – of two plants together so that they fuse to create one single specimen. The plant which is supplying the root system is known as the stock; the variety – which must be a close botanical relative – to be attached to this is called the scion. Once the scion has begun to grow away – usually after a growing season – all the foliage and branches (the head) of the stock is cut off and prevented from further growth. And that's all there is to it!

Simple though the principle is, success with grafting can be a little elusive, especially to

SHIELD BUDDING A ROOTSTOCK

1. During summer select a healthy shoot of bud wood – the material from which the bud will be removed – and remove leaves, leaving the stalks.
2. Cut off a leaf axil with bud. 3. Remove the remaining tiny sliver of wood in the bark. 4. Cut a T-shaped incision in the stock plant. 5. Insert the bud and bind cleanly and securely, using raffia. 6. The stock can be cut back when the scion has grown – usually a season later.

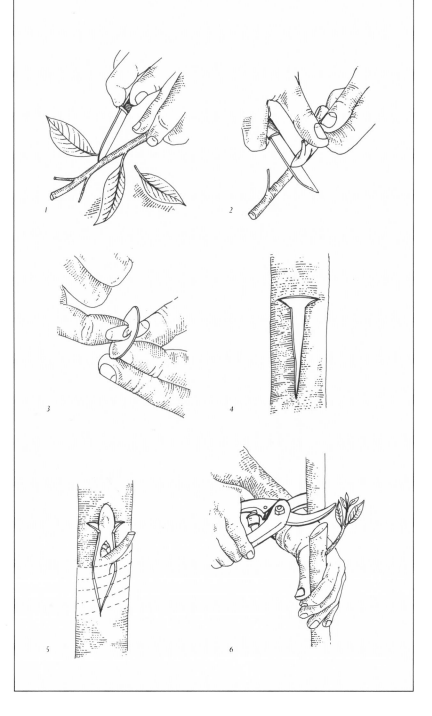

amateur gardeners. There is much literature on the subject, from the semi-mythical reports of Pliny the elder, in Roman times, to the highly technical papers emanating from today's research stations, but throughout, the same principles apply. The graft is effected by making a wound in the skin of one plant and cutting off a shoot or at least a bud of the other and then binding their vital tissues together so that they merge as quickly as possible. Since infection could easily invade such a vulnerable spot, cleanliness and deftness of operation are all-important, minimizing the extent of the wound but maximizing the area of contact between the two living tissues. As Mrs Loudon wrote in *Gardening for Ladies* in 1846: 'This is an operation that requires the greatest nicety and exactness; as, unless the inner bark of the bud fits quite closely to the soft wood of the stock, it is in vain to hope that it will take.'

Budding is one of the simplest methods of grafting and is particularly useful for introducing new varieties of roses on to root-stocks. In midsummer, a slip of bark which carries a dormant bud is inserted into a T-shaped slit at the base of the stem of the stock plant. The union is then sealed with special grafting wax or bound in with raffia. Historically, beeswax or clean clay was used to make the seal. Within a few months, the bud should 'take' – that is, fuse with the tissues of the stock and shoot into new growth.

Other kinds of grafting are normally carried out while the plants are dormant, but late enough in winter to avoid the worst excesses of frost. There are several ways in which the scion can be attached to the stock.

Whip and tongue grafting is one of the simplest and most widely used methods for grafting a variety on to a young rootstock, and is used for apples, pears and many ornamental trees. The saddle grafting system works particularly well for rhododendrons. Spliced side grafting is similar to saddle grafting except that the scion is fixed at one side of the stock, rather than as a saddle, and veneer grafting (also known as inarching) is similar to the spliced side method, except that the stock is left uncut until the scion has taken and is growing. Both are useful for grafting conifers.

Grafting may seem complicated, but, in practice, it is relatively simple, once the basic

Fruit trees, such as these 'Worcester Pearmain' apples, are most commonly propagated by whip and tongue grafting when they are young – with this method of grafting, it is important that the stock and scion are about the same diameter.

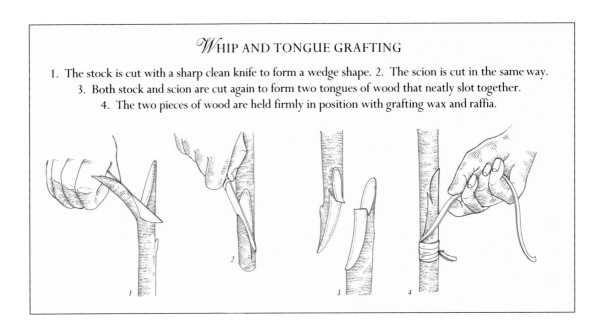

WHIP AND TONGUE GRAFTING

1. The stock is cut with a sharp clean knife to form a wedge shape. 2. The scion is cut in the same way.
3. Both stock and scion are cut again to form two tongues of wood that neatly slot together.
4. The two pieces of wood are held firmly in position with grafting wax and raffia.

skills have been acquired. It is essential to be well equipped, with a clean, sharp grafting or budding knife, to use only healthy stocks and scions, and to make more grafts than you need, on the assumption that they will not all take.

During the eighteenth and nineteenth centuries it was also common to graft plants together as they grew, particularly for example, in formal plantings of trees, where they might be both pleached and grafted together to make a more solid screen. By today's standards, the results might be considered rather unnatural, but it would not be difficult to carry out, if you have the space and the time to graft and bind the branches together.

Cuttings

Grafting demands considerable skill and patience but anyone can root cuttings. Indeed, it is often success with a snippet of houseplant that kindles the flame of enthusiasm in a new gardener! The amazing resilience and versatility of the plant kingdom is never more apparent than when seemingly doomed, rootless pieces of stem can rest in contact with the earth, grow roots and develop into a whole new individual.

Cuttings have been raised since time immemorial. Theophrastus wrote about them 400 years before the birth of Christ and the rules that applied in those days still hold today. To succeed, cuttings need to root as quickly as possible, preferably before the meagre reserve of nutrients in the cut stem expires. To effect this, wilting must be minimized by ensuring that the atmosphere around the cuttings is kept as moist as possible without rot setting in. To develop roots, the stems need to be in close contact with the rooting medium and must be kept absolutely still.

There are two main types of cuttings: young or soft shoots, taken during the growing season, and woody or mature slips, usually taken during the dormant period.

SOFT CUTTINGS

Soft cuttings root quickly but need more attention than woody or ripe slips. One traditional method was to place a small pot inside a large one and to fill the space between the two with potting compost. The cuttings were then inserted into the compost, taking care to trim off the lower leaves so that none came into contact with the compost. Water was poured into the empty centre pot, whose drainage hole was suitably plugged, so that the compost could be moistened without becoming water-logged. Finally, a bell jar was placed over the whole lot.

An alternative was simply to place cuttings directly in the ground and to place the bell jar over them. From then on, it was the management of the equipment that mattered. 'Some cuttings when thus treated,' wrote Mrs Loudon (1846) 'are very apt to damp off, and require to have the glass taken up occasionally, and wiped.' Thus, the air surrounding the plants was kept at maximum humidity to minimize wilting while ensuring that any condensation which could initiate the rot was removed.

It has been known for centuries that most cuttings root faster in warm soil than in cool, so the application of 'bottom heat' is by no means a new idea, even if the electric soil-warming cable is a relatively new innovation. Before electricity, other means were used to supply heat, such as hot water pipes or special kerosene heaters, but the most natural method, and one which will still work, was the hotbed (see page 21). Fresh dung was piled up to provide a source of heat and a frame sometimes placed over it. Rather than pushing cuttings directly into the hotbed, Mrs Loudon (1846) recommends plunging in the pots in which they have been planted. This makes later handling easier and more pleasant.

As long as the cuttings look fresh, they are doing well, but any yellowing or, worse, blackening of the foliage, should be removed along with any dead cuttings. All the old writers agree on this, and on the need to pot up plants as soon as they have begun to grow.

The old-fashioned double wallflower 'Harpur Crewe' can only be propagated by taking cuttings. These ten-week-old plants were rooted in a propagator with bottom heat and are now, in midsummer, ready to be planted out.

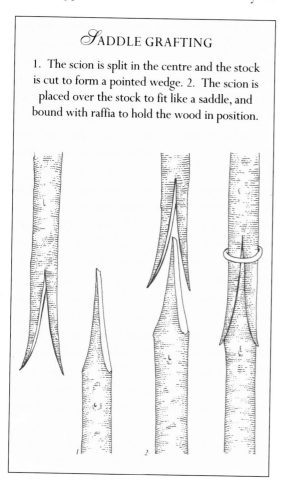

ℐADDLE GRAFTING

1. The scion is split in the centre and the stock is cut to form a pointed wedge. 2. The scion is placed over the stock to fit like a saddle, and bound with raffia to hold the wood in position.

Half-ripe Cuttings

A wide range of shrubby plants are propagated by taking half-ripe cuttings in mid- to late summer and may either be cut or torn to include a woody strip. Treat as for soft cuttings.

The choice of potting compost varies according to which plants are being struck. Modern peat-based, or peat-free, composts have little in common with the ancient mixtures, but their mode of action is much the same and there is little to be gained, therefore, in slavishly copying the old recipes. Silver sand was widely used as an aid to drainage, and with plants that are likely to rot, powdered or ground charcoal was often mixed in. This absorbed malodorous gases generated by decomposing plant material and thus helped to keep the compost sweet. Cuttings of dry-land plants such as pinks and carnations were often struck in pure sand, as were heathers which might otherwise have rotted. Then as now, it seems, different people found that different methods suited different plants. 'The great object,' says Mrs Loudon (1846), 'is to excite and stimulate the plant.'

The great boon of modern propagation has been the introduction of hormone rooting compound. This speeds up the rate at which the severed stems callous and develop roots, thereby reducing the length of that vulnerable period when the dreaded rot can invade or when unattended plants can dry out. The only

possible substitute for hormone rooting compound is careful management and you must be prepared for your cuttings to take longer to develop. There is one way of almost cheating, however. All willow species root with amazing rapidity because they are especially rich in hormones which stimulate root development. An infusion of chopped willow twigs and cold water is said, therefore, to hasten the rate at which the cuttings which are dipped in it will root. I cannot say whether this is universally effective or not, but it has to be less unpleasant than the ancient Roman trick of dipping the stems of their cuttings into pure cattle manure before planting them!

WOODY CUTTINGS

The propagating method for woody cuttings is much simpler than with vulnerable soft growth. They are taken at a quiet time of year when there is no growth to speak of and everything is happening much more slowly. Young but woody stems are cut from parent plants and pushed into the ground where, in the right conditions, they will quietly develop

Chrysanthemums are raised from basal cuttings in the most vigorous plants; the cuttings are removed from last season's stools (roots), which are stimulated into growth by application of gentle heat in the greenhouse. Blooms like these result from laborious removal of all side buds.

Hardwood Cuttings

1. In autumn, select young woody stems that have ripened – turned woody this season. Remove any surplus growth and cut into 23 cm (9 in) lengths.
2. Insert into gritty compost and set in a cold frame or a cool part of the greenhouse.

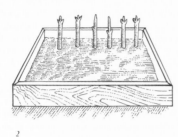

Alternatively: 1. Place the hardwood cuttings in a slit trench in the garden.
2. Rooted plants will be ready to transplant one season later.

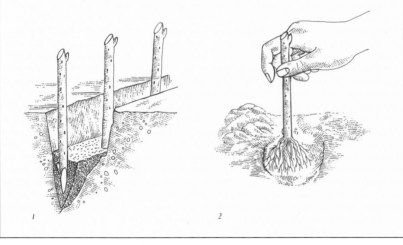

roots over a period of about six months and then sprout. It is amusing to think that this might be the basis for legends of the staves of such people as the biblical Joseph of Arimathea whose staff grew into a tree, or of Tannhäuser, if you're a Wagner fan, whose staff miraculously sprouted leaves and flowers, but, as a general rule, only the youngest whips will sprout. There are some exceptions to this rule: olives will grow from mature cuttings, and here is Mrs Loudon's (1846) description of rooting mulberries from what she calls 'truncheons': 'If a large limb of a [mulberry] tree be cut off, and stuck into the ground, it will grow without any further trouble being taken with it; and probably the next year, or the year after, it will bear an abundance of fruit.'

Ideal conditions for woody cuttings consist of a reasonably constant temperature and moist soil which does not dry out. Plants which are especially easy to propagate this way include many of the more vigorous shrubs, particularly willows, viburnums, forsythias, some lilacs and shrub roses. If you are planning to plant a hedge, this is a simple and inexpensive, if rather time-consuming, way of propagating such hedging plants as privet or box. It is unrealistic, however, to expect to grow the hedge from scratch in position simply by pushing sticks into the ground. A better method is to root the cuttings in one specially favourable area, where temperatures are reasonably constant and the soil is in good order and, at the same time, prepare and feed the soil where the hedge is to run, transplanting the young hedge plants when they are ready during winter.

The hardiest woody plants will root in open ground, but most of them benefit from extra shelter. The modern method is to dig a narrow trench, insert the cuttings in a row and then to cover these with a low tunnel of clear plastic, stretched over a series of hoops. Before the age of plastic, similar results could be achieved with cloches, or by simply heaping bales of straw round the cuttings to create protection.

Selection of material for cuttings is important. Young plants yield stems that will root much more readily than those from older specimens. Mrs Loudon (1846) also suggests that stems situated nearest to the ground root more readily than those located higher up the bush. The best rose cuttings come from a long, vigorous, unbranched wand (one year's growth), which can be cut into several pieces, each about 25 cm (10 in) long. (Make sure

" *For* the seeds sound and good, do yeild after the sowing plants of the like goodnesse and vertue. "

Thomas Hill, 1652

these are pushed into the ground the right way round! If you find it hard to tell, look for the leaf scar and notice that the tiny axillary bud is above the scar.)

As soon as the woody cuttings are growing strongly, their old stems should be cut back to the lowest bud to ensure vigorous new growth and an evenly shaped plant. If they are not to be potted, they should be left *in situ* until the following autumn, by which time good-sized plants will have developed.

Seeds and seeding

Seed is nature's way of propagating most plants and, even for shrubs and trees which grow more slowly, it is still one of the best ways of producing healthy, vigorous offspring. Exceptions, of course, are seed-sterile varieties and clones, which must be propagated vegetatively to keep pure. Annuals, on the other hand, can only be reproduced by seed and most perennials, even those that do not come true from seed, are well worth raising from seed, especially if the resulting progeny is to go through a further selection process and subsequent improvement of stock.

COLLECTING AND STORING

There are, of course, hundreds of firms marketing seed to amateur growers, but it can also be deeply satisfying to produce and sow your own and to organize swaps with fellow gardeners – again, a traditional practice popular with old-time gardeners.

Collecting-time for seed varies from plant to plant, but generally it stretches from late spring, when some of the earliest flowers will be seeding, to late autumn, when the last of the autumn perennials ripen. Before cleaning or extracting the seed, plant material should be stored in a dry, airy place that is reasonably cool. One advantage our forebears had over us is that their dwellings tended to be more roomy. How many of today's houses can boast an apple loft or a cool, roomy cellar? Nineteenth-century gardeners hung up all manner of plants, the flowerheads carefully inserted into paper bags, and left them to dry slowly so that their seed ripened and fell for later retrieval, at which time they were packeted and stored in the coolest part of the house until sowing time. In most modern houses, a corner of a cool cupboard or possibly part of the garage has to serve, but it is important to guard against rodents and birds stealing seed,

Left and below: Collecting seed is a simple and rather enjoyable procedure that enables gardeners to ensure a continuation of their favourite lines. Modern F_1 hybrids will not come true from seed, but most of the older vegetables and flowers do. Some truly vintage varieties are almost unobtainable commercially, and their survival may depend on enthusiasts sharing seed on a private basis.

and seed must be protected against damp and spoiling.

A good many species will produce reasonably clean seed straight from the plant. Among the annuals, marigolds, candytufts and most of the pea family will, for example, yield ripe seed straight into the hand. Be warned, however, that saving seed of F_1 hybrids can be futile. Many modern hybrids are sterile and produce only infertile seed, or the progeny will be vastly inferior to the parent. Poppy heads can be plucked and shaken, like a pepper pot, into an open envelope. Perennials like aquilegias and hellebores can be handled in the same way, but you need to keep a sharp eye open, because once their pods have split, their seed is shed quickly and you may arrive too late.

Plants with especially fleshy fruits, such as irises, tulips or fritillaries, can be plucked just as the pods are about to split and inserted into a roomy paper bag where the drying process can finish off without the seed getting scattered and lost. Primulas, too, need picking *before* their capsules open and are dried in the same way.

Some species have a cunning way of catapulting their seed, when you least expect it, or of using aerodynamics to disperse themselves. Clematis and anemone seed can blow away in a puff of breeze and cranesbills (*Geranium*) has spring-loaded capsules which refuse to be violated when unripe, but which flick their ripe seeds with an audible 'ping', usually before you can get at them. These are the tricky ones and, oddly enough, little guidance is given in the old literature as to how seed from such species can be safely collected. The secret is to be early, catching the plant before the capsules are fully ripened. Cut with plenty of stem to allow the ripening process to continue after harvest and hang the plants upside down in a bag so that the seed won't propel itself across the floor.

Cleaning harvested seed is a laborious process but an advisable one, particularly if you

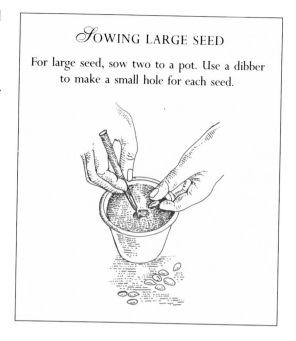

Sowing Large Seed

For large seed, sow two to a pot. Use a dibber to make a small hole for each seed.

plan to exchange seed with others. With most types of seed, it is relatively easy to shake the seeds plus any debris out on to a clean sheet of paper and blow *gently* until the chaff has blown away. Large seeds can be graded out of the dross by using a paper knife or a metal ruler, stroking them to one side repeatedly until the chaff is separated. Then, all that remains is the packeting. For exchange, you may wish to use small envelopes, which should be labelled with the plant variety of the parent, its provenance, date of harvest and any other useful information. For seeds packeted for your own purposes, old mail envelopes serve just as well as new ones and cost nothing.

Seed should be stored cool, dry and preferably dark until needed for sowing. Seed life varies from a few months to many years, depending on species, but a safe rule is to be sure to sow fresh!

SOWING OUTSIDE

Although different seed needs different treatment, as a general rule the seeds of most hardy annuals, herbaceous perennials and vegetables will germinate quite happily without artificial

A species of 'orange peel' clematis from the Himalayas with tufty seedheads.

Right: when planting leeks, make a trench with the side of the hoe, running parallel with the garden line.

Far right: holes are made for the leeks using a dibber and the leeks planted deep enough to cover the white parts of the stem. Be sure to fill each hole with water.

heat, whereas tender plants, even though they are destined to be grown outdoors, will germinate much more easily with bottom heat.

Sowing outdoors, without heat, directly into the ground is the simplest method of raising seeds, but all writers on the subject stress the importance of soil preparation for successful germination. New young plants need to be able to penetrate the soil easily, so a friable, moist tilth is essential. Some seeds, lettuce for example, need light to germinate, so planting deeply is injurious, and as a general rule seed should be sown in shallow drills.

For most seeds, the soil should be warm for sowing, since below 7°C (45°F) few seeds will germinate. Apparently, before the age of thermometers, explain Maureen and Bridget Boland in *Old Wives' Lore for Gardeners* (1976), farmers in Lincolnshire in England used to take down their trousers and sit on the soil in order to test the temperature; if it felt comfortable, the ground was ready for sowing. For the modern gardener, the Misses Boland suggest that an elbow test will suffice!

However, some seeds will germinate more easily if they are exposed to frost, in a process

SOWING SEED

1. Fill a tray with seed-sowing compost. This should be a light, friable material without added nutrients. Level off the surface, removing surplus material. 2. Firm the surface gently. Do not tamp down too hard. 3. Sprinkle seed sparingly over the surface of the soil. For seed that does not require light for germination, cover with a fine layer of compost or grit. 4. If warmth is required, cover sown trays with a pane of glass under which a sheet of paper has been spread. Remove this as soon as germination has commenced.

1   *2*   *3*   *4*

old gardeners called stratification. It is a method particularly suited to species from regions where winters are hard and where autumn germination could prove fatal. As a natural defence, the seed coat is so tough that it will only crack after a hard frost, thereby ensuring spring germination. The seeds are placed in shallow pans or boxes, covered with a layer of sand and some fine-mesh wire netting to protect the contents from mice, and then put out of doors in an exposed position throughout the winter. The seeds are sown in the ordinary way the following spring.

An old gardening tip for speeding up germination once seeds have been sown comes from Bernard Schofield (*A Miscellany of Garden Wisdom*, 1991). Fill a fine rose sprinkler with hot water and give the new seeds an initial watering. Use tepid water thereafter.

SOWING INSIDE

Sowing inside in pans is still carried on today as it has been for centuries. The modern plastic seed tray is in fact no better and certainly not as long-lasting as the clay seed pan or the less expensive wooden seed flat. The best of the clay seed pans have sloping sides, drainage holes in the bottom and are deep enough to accommodate sufficient compost to avoid drying out too quickly. Into the bottom of such pans, broken crock is placed – to assist drainage – and this is then covered with a seed compost. Nowadays, peat-based or other organic mixes are routinely used, but before World War I, potting composts were made up from such raw materials as sand, loam and leafmould. Perennial and tree or shrub seeds can be sown on to these and covered with a fine layer of grit before placing them into a cold frame (see page 117), preferably uncovered but protected from the worst of the wind, until germination takes place. With some plants this may take months and so care needs to be taken to prevent the

growth of fungus moulds and mosses on the compost surface.

Nowadays, with electric propagators making life so easy, we tend to forget what trouble gardeners had in order to provide annual seeds with adequate heat, before the advent of cheap energy. Here is the method recommended by the *Annals of Horticulture* of 1846: 'Dig out a trench three feet [60cm] wide and eighteen inches [46 cm] deep, fill it with hot stable dung, treading it down so as to leave three inches [7.5 cm] thickness for mould [leaf mould] to fill it up level; upon this sow your seed under hand-glasses.'

The advantage that old clay pans and wooden seed flats have over modern plastic is that they can be used year after year without deterioration. But, unlike plastic, they are not easy to clean and, for hygiene purposes, must be scrubbed well before being reused.

Left: throughout history, gardeners have known that young plants are particularly vulnerable after being potted up, so the aftercare needs to be diligent. These young seedlings will overwinter under glass and be ready to plant out next spring.

Below: seedlings that have been hardened off can be planted in the garden – in this case, into a space where an earlier crop has been removed.

Wallflowers, traditionally grown from seed in the kitchen garden, are planted out in flower beds in the autumn. The plants should be stocky with plenty of branches.

Once seedlings have germinated and emerged, the next step is to prick them out, trying not to disturb the roots too much, and then to plant them in pots to grow on until large enough to line out in the nursery or plant out in the borders outdoors.

The most common problems with seedling aftercare have always been connected with water. Clean water is important in the early stages to avoid the disease of 'damping off', but, according to several writers of the nineteenth century, the quality of water dictated to a considerable extent how well the plants would do. Pond water was regarded kindly because it was thought to contain nutrients from decayed material. Rain water was fine, especially when it had a chance to sit about and climb to room, or rather greenhouse, temperature, but spring water, cold from the bowels of the earth, was considered distinctly bad. Oddly enough, the same advice would hold today, except that instead of spring water, the produce that comes along our water mains is usually rich in chlorine and should, ideally, stand for an hour or two before being used.

After transplanting young subjects into open ground, nineteenth-century gardeners were in the habit of shading them with leafy branches or hessian, to avoid wilting while they developed a root system. This practice is not seen much nowadays, but it is an excellent technique for hastening plant establishment, particularly in areas where spring sun is fierce or spring winds keen and dry.

SELECTION

One of the curses of modern nursery techniques is mass production. The nurseryman of old, and many keen gardeners, were in the habit of planting out many more seedlings of perennial plants than they really needed. They would then allow them all to flower and would make a selection of the best. Thus, each nursery would offer vegetatively reproduced stock of their own selected seedlings. In private gardens, this is a simple and enjoyable process, ensuring a gradual improvement in quality. There is no need, of course, to select every species, but certain plants, especially those which seed easily, are simple to improve upon and give speedy results.

Gertrude Jekyll made repeated selections of polyanthus primulas, for example, gradually developing and improving the purity of her strains of creams and yellows. With free-seeding biennials such as foxgloves, selection can be based on colour, height, flower habit and so on until a distinctive group develops. The most famous of selections of this kind was, perhaps, the Reverend Wilks's work on British wild field poppies to produce the strain of soft pastel shades of his Shirley poppies.

Simple methods of propagation

If the foregoing methods of propagation seem over-complicated or time-consuming, there are, fortunately, a number of other simpler, but nevertheless effective, systems of propagation which have been employed since ancient times.

DIVISION

Plants with a creeping rootstock, such as bergamot, perennial asters and bellflowers, or those which form a thick fibrous base, such as primroses, sedums and heucheras, from which many stems arise, can be divided. Division is still one of the most effective ways of bulking up perennials, indeed, most perennials actually *need* to be regularly divided to perform properly. The procedure as laid down over the centuries is simply to lift the plant, preferably in the dormant season, tear it to pieces and then replant the pieces. The initial division is easiest to show by illustrating two forks being

The glorious herbaceous borders of the 1890s depended on regular division and replanting of the perennials. These Hemerocallis, *once replanted, will grow with renewed vigour for about three seasons when the whole process will need to be repeated.*

used to prise the plant apart. This has become one of the most widely used clichés in garden writing and, even though it does explain what to do with fine pictorial succinctness, it fails to explain that the smaller the ultimate divisions are, the more vigorously they will grow. In practice, my own technique is more brutal than the two-fork system, and consists of chopping the plants with a spade, or tearing portions off with my bare hands!

LAYERING

Propagation by layering calls for a gentler touch. The idea is to persuade a plant to start producing roots at a point along its stem so that it can be separated eventually from its parent. As with so many instructions, Mrs Loudon (1846) expresses it with near perfect clarity: 'The only art required in layering is to

Much of the old horticultural literature concerns itself with how to induce plants to sprout roots from a submerged stem and hence develop an entirely new plant. Climbers such as clematis lend themselves to this ancient propagation technique – popular with amateur gardeners, because it requires minimal skill and almost no equipment.

contrive the most effectual means of interrupting the returning sap, so as to produce as great an accumulation of it as possible at the joint from which the roots are to be produced.' This is affected by cutting or scraping half-way through the young stem, which is then submerged in the ground. Mrs Loudon suggests holding the wound open with a matchstick-sized splint, but in practice, as long as the stem has been wounded and is firmly anchored into a soil that has been made conducive to rooting by adding a little peat or compost, vigorous rooting is almost inevitable.

More than one plant can be layered from the same shoot by pegging it down in series with an anchor at each bud – this is serpentine layering.

Air layering This is also known as Chinese Layering, and was widely practised in the 1840s in Europe and North America, especially

LAYERING

1. Select a branch near to the ground and bend this downwards, taking care not to break it. 2. Make a small cut in the bark or scrape away some of the bark before laying it down in a shallow hole in the soil. 3. Add compost to enrich the soil that you replace in the hole. Peg down the branch with a wire loop, or weight it down with a stone.

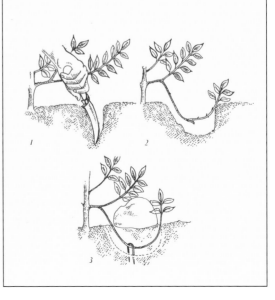

SERPENTINE LAYERING

Extra long stems can be wounded at intervals, covered with soil and anchored down with stones or wire pegs. Roots and new plants will be produced within a season. Serpentine layering is suitable for most shrubs and climbers with long pliable stems.

Layering in the nineteenth century, 'by circumposition'.

Strawberries layer themselves prolifically, but a useful shortcut is to allow the runners to root directly into a flower pot filled with compost. The resulting plants can then be transplanted at any time without risk of damage to the roots.

with indoor fruits such as oranges, and with camellias. Nowadays, it is a speedy way of propagating woody house plants such as *Ficus* or *Monstera*, but works well for some outdoor shrubs as well. The old method was to cut the side out of a flowerpot and wedge the branch of the plant in question, having first cut a ring incision into the bark, into the pot, which was then packed with wet moss. A safer alternative, used by Baron Humboldt in Latin America, was to cut a ring in the bark of the branch to be layered, and then to pack damp soil over the wound and hold this in place with oil cloth, which was tightly sealed to keep the moisture

in. After about three months, the roots will penetrate the oil cloth.

The modern adaptation of this ancient technique is simply to replace the moist earth with potting compost or a mix of sphagnum moss and compost and to seal it in with clear plastic. When the roots become visible, the branch is ready to be detached from the mother plant.

AIR LAYERING

1. Make a single cut half-way across the stem of the plant to be layered. 2. Pack moss or compost around the wound. 3. Hold this in place using polythene or plastic tied at either end. 4. Remove the young plant when the roots have appeared.

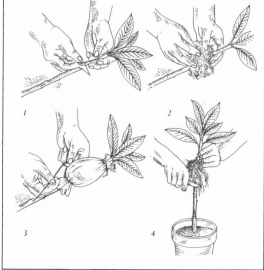

STOOLING

This is a time-honoured nursery technique and a simple but effective way of making more plants. Stooling works for a great many perennials and shrubs, especially those with large numbers of basal shoots, such as raspberries, flowering currants, herbaceous clematis, forsythia and viburnums. The plants are encouraged to produce roots along the lower parts of their stems by piling enriched soil up around the bases of the plants during winter and leaving it there for a growing season. After the roots have developed, the soil is moved away from the plants, and the stems – each with its shock of new roots – are cut off and transplanted for growing on.

Pollination

Apples, pears and plums always fruit more efficiently when two or more compatible varieties are grown together so that bees can transfer pollen from one to the other.

In small gardens, or where space is restricted, it is possible to graft different varieties to the same stock for cross-pollination. In some areas, nurseries even offer so-called 'family trees' with three or more compatible varieties ready-grafted.

The choice of old-fashioned methods of propagation is, then, still as wide as ever. It is unlikely there will ever be a less expensive way of expanding a plant collection than by home-propagating and anyone who wants to cultivate an interesting garden, old-fashioned or not, owes it to themselves to become efficient propagators.

Though many commercial nurseries have installed elaborate hospital-like facilities to propagate varieties of perennials and woody plants by 'tissue culture', plants raised by this method can show some variation from the parent, and are more easily lost during the weaning period from tissue to pot culture than old-fashioned methods of propagation such as root division and cuttings.

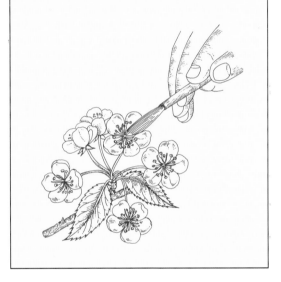

*H*AND-POLLINATING

Open flowers of fruiting plants such as peaches, tomatoes or, in this case, pears, can be pollinated by brushing the stamens with a soft brush or piece of wool. This is only necessary with indoor crops, since, in a well-balanced garden, insects will do the work outdoors.

In a glasshouse, where there are few bees, fruits such as peaches, nectarines or apricots must be hand-pollinated. Traditionally, a camel hair brush, rabbit's paw or tuft of wool was used, the job being made easier here by tying the tuft to a bamboo cane.

Soil and cultivation

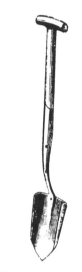

Garden spade, 1859

These young vegetables – runner beans, peas and broad beans – are getting off to a good start. Gardeners have always recognized that success depends on the careful preparation of the soil and then keeping it in as good a condition as possible.

$\mathscr{M}$odern science has opened a whole series of new windows on the importance of soil. We know now, for example, that not only is all healthy soil teaming with life from micro-organisms, including fungi, nematodes, and small invertebrates, but also that many of those organisms have a close relationship with specific plants so that the one cannot thrive without the other. Terrestrial orchids, for example, need mycorrhiza – a fungal association among their roots – to thrive. Pulses enjoy an enhanced supply of nitrogen thanks to nitrogen-fixing bacteria in their root nodules. We also have a much fuller grasp of the role that mineral nutrients play,

not only the major ones – such as phosphates and potash – but also trace elements such as copper, manganese and iron.

Ancient gardeners had only a rudimentary knowledge of minerals plants needed and they understood little of soil science. But they had a thorough understanding of the conditions plants needed in order to thrive, what would make them grow with more gusto, and what defects would cause problems. We know that, to work properly, soil must contain a mixture of mineral particles, organic matter, air and water in which mineral nutrients are dissolved. Our forebears knew that soil needed to be light and friable, that added compost and dung not only enriched it but also improved its texture, and that if the land was not free-draining, plants would not develop root systems. Put simplistically, modern science tells us why but the ancients knew *how*.

The soil

'. . . the Gardener by taking up a clod of earth, should esely trie the goodness of it after this manner: in considering whether the earth be neither hot and bare, not leane by sand, lacking a mixture of perfect earth: nor the same found to be wholly chalk, not naughty sand: nor barren gravel, nor of the glistering pouder or dust of a leane stony ground, not the earth continual moist; for all these be the special defaults of a good and perfect earth.'

So wrote Thomas Hill in the sixteenth century, echoing an age-old concern to identify

the quality of the soil with which the gardener had to work. There are five main types of soil: sand, silt, chalk (limestone or alkaline) soil, clay and peat. However, soils are often a mixture of these five different types and they are then described as loams. A heavy loam contains a high proportion of clay; a medium loam, which is a mixture of clay, silt and sand, is the closest to an ideal working soil. Medium loam usually contains a good supply of plant foods, drains well, and is fairly easy to work.

It is easy to identify what kind of soil you have by look and touch: get hold of a handful of earth and see how it feels and observe its colour. An additional check recommended by Walter P. Wright in *Scientific & Practical Gardening* (1938) is to identify the wild flowers growing in your area; they are a good indication of soil type. The basic soil types are described below, but Thomas Hill's advice on soil improvement still holds good today: 'If the earth shall be found naughty or unfruitful, as the clayie, sandy, and chalkie, then ought the same to be amended, after the mind of the skilfull, with marle and dung laid three foot [90 cm] deepe, and well turned in with earth: if this be perceived over thin and leane, then to be mixed and holpen by a fat earth: or to a barren and over drie ground, may be mixed a moist and very fat earth. A watery ground is made the better, if the same be mixed with a sandy or smal gravelly earth, and deep Allies made, for the conveying and shifting of the water falling in the night.'

Sand Wild flowers that naturally thrive on a sandy soil include catchfly (*Silene nutans*), spurry (*Spergula arvensis*), evening primrose (*Oenothera biennis*) and cornflower (*Centaurea cyanus*). Gorse

Vegetable allotments often exhibit model gardening with good stewardship of the soil and skilled crop husbandry.

141

Top: most poppy species will thrive and multiply prolifically on any free-draining soil.

Above: most viburnums enjoy alkaline soils and several species, like this Viburnum tinus, *flower in the winter.*

(*Ulex europaeus*), broom (*Cytisus* sp.), and poppies (*Papaver rhoeas*) also like a sandy soil. A sandy soil has a light, gritty texture and is easy to work. Because it is porous, water runs away too quickly, removing plant foods from the soil. Sandy soils therefore need regular feeding with manure and compost if any improvement is to be seen.

Chalk (Limestone or alkaline soil) Identifying wild flowers include chicory (*Cichorium intybus*), bladder campion (*Silene vulgaris*), bird's-foot trefoil (*Lotus corniculatus*), and kidney vetch (*Anthyllis vulneraria*). Box (*Buxus* sp.), yew (*Taxus baccata*), viburnums (*Viburnum* sp.), dogwood (*Cornus* sp.), clematis (*Clematis* sp.), and clovers (*Trifolium* sp.) in grass are other indications of a chalky soil. Not surprisingly, a chalky soil looks pale and crumbles easily in the hand. Like sandy soil, it does not hold moisture well, and therefore loses plant foods easily. Hill, for example, dismisses it out of hand: 'But worst of all others is that ground, which shall be both drie and grosse, lean and cold. In the kinds of ground, the chalk is to be refused.' It is true that very chalky soils also cause a mineral deficiency in some plants, the typical symptoms being that the leaves turn yellow. This is basically because the soil 'locks in' certain plant foods, notably iron, magnesium and potassium, which are then unavailable to plants. The traditional method to reduce this problem was to apply plenty of dung and leafmould on a regular basis, and this system would still work well for the gardener today.

Clay A marked population of the following wild flowers indicate a clay soil: coltsfoot (*Tussilago farfara*), common and corn sowthistle (*Sonchus oleraceus* and *S. arvensis*), and buttercup (*Ranunculus acris*). Oak (*Quercus* sp.) trees, willows (*Salix* sp.) and elders (*Sambucus*) also like a clay soil, as do forget-me-nots (*Myosotis* sp.), coneflowers (*Rudbeckia* sp.), and mimulus (*Mimulus* sp.). A clay soil is subject to extremes,

although it retains plant foods well. In wet weather it becomes heavy and sticky, and the surface of the soil is greasy to the touch. In hot, dry weather, it becomes completely parched, baked to a hard surface which cracks. Drainage is obviously a problem, and this can be improved by frequent digging, adding well-rotted stable or farmyard manure, or leafmould, which will also aerate the soil. If this is done in midwinter, the weather can also assist here. Leave the surface of the soil rough for frost action to break it up. Acid clay soils benefit from a sprinkling of lime (see page 144).

Silt For identifying plants, see clay above. A silty soil is made up of very small particles, which gives it its familiar grainy texture. Like clay, it easily becomes waterlogged, but drainage can be improved by regular applications of well-rotted manure and compost.

Peat A peaty soil is usually acidic, making it the ideal soil for acid-loving plants such as azaleas (*Azalea* sp.), rhododendrons (*Rhododendron* sp.) and heathers (*Erica* sp.). Peat is very deep brown or dark grey in colour and has a spongy texture. It is rich in humus, but not in nutrients, and may benefit from the application of organic compound fertilizers such as blood, fish and bone meal, or seaweed meal. In order to grow a wide range of plants, peat will need to be limed (see page 144).

HUMUS

Humus consists of organic matter in the process of decay. It has a fine, sticky texture, and is

The key to success in food growing is to work continuously at improving the soil. The dark colour and texture of this earth shows that it has been well fed for many years.

red hot. As soon as the soil was cool, it was weighed once more and if there had been a further appreciable loss, this indicated a fair proportion of humus in the soil.

To test the soil's water-holding capacity, Wright suggests placing a sample of soil in a jar of water (he recommends using rainwater in a hard-water area). The jar is then shaken and a note made of how much coarse sand sinks to the bottom. The rest of the water is placed in separate jars and a note made of how quickly the finer particles settle. The longer the particles take to rest, the more clay there is in the soil. A high incidence of coarse sand will indicate a soil that dries out quickly.

Another way to check the richness of humus in your soil is to look at the worms. Fat, red, glistening worms exist in good soils. If the worms are greyish-red and slow-moving with a tendency to curl, then the soil needs help.

Weeds are also a good indication of the state of the soil. Chickweed shows that there is plenty of nitrogen in the soil. Nettles grow well in humus-rich soil, but not so well in soil that contains a high proportion of chalk, sand or stones. Fat hen, or white goosefoot, grows well on a light loamy soil in which there is a good supply of plant foods.

None of these experiments or observations will, of course, conclusively establish the plant food levels of your soil, but they will give you a rough indication. If you prefer, you can buy a do-it-yourself kit to test the soil for nutrients, although this will not be as accurate as sending a sample of soil away to a professional laboratory for analysis.

ALKALINE AND ACID SOILS

Most plants grow best in a slightly acid to neutral soil (pH 6.5 to pH 7.0), and problems can occur if the soil is too acid or alkaline. A soil-testing kit is the most accurate way to measure the pH value of your soil, although

dark brown or black in colour, with a pleasant, sweet smell. Humus provides the right conditions for bacteria to multiply, which in turn break down a number of the complex chemicals found in organic matter into readily available plant foods. Humus also acts like a sponge, retaining moisture and at the same time assisting drainage. A soil with a high content of humus is what Thomas Hill would have called 'a fertil, commodious and well yeilding ground' that 'require a sweetness to consist in it, which the Gardener shall easily find and know by tast of it'. Hill recommends that the gardener check the sweetness of the soil by placing a little on the tip of the tongue, by which 'he shall incontinent feele and perceive ... of what condition the same is'. If this doesn't appeal, Walter P. Wright (1938) suggested the following scientific experiment for schools in the 1930s to gauge the amount of humus in the soil. A sample of soil was taken from midway down in the topsoil and a note made of its weight. The sample was then left to dry in the sun, weighed again and placed in a very hot oven to dry it out further. After weighing it again, the soil was placed on a metal sheet and heated over an open flame until the soil was plants naturally growing in your area will give some indication of soil condition. For example, acid soils (below pH 7.0) favour heathers, rhododendrons, camellias, pine trees, and azaleas. Yew trees, viburnums, dogwoods, and clematis are some of the plants that will grow on alkaline soils (above pH 7.0).

Acid soils are easier to adjust than alkaline soils, simply by the application of lime (see below). Alkaline soils need large amounts of well-rotted manure, composts or leafmould applied on a regular basis to counteract the excessive amounts of lime.

Lime The importance of liming has long been understood and burnt lime or quicklime (calcium oxide) has been applied to neutralize high acid soils in fields and garden plots since Roman times. As a soil conditioner, lime has long been considered important in assisting clay soils to flocculate – to bind smaller particles to form larger ones, making a more open structure – and, indeed, its physiological functions – aiding the absorption of minerals by certain plants – are by no means a twentieth-century discovery.

The amount of lime you need depends on the acidity of the soil and the soil type. The soil-testing kit will give advice about the amount of lime needed. It is important to follow the guidelines since, once applied, lime takes centuries to leach out of the soil. Thus, if lime-hating ornamentals – rhododendrons or camellias, for example – are grown on naturally acid soil that has been limed, they will languish. In the days of Henry VIII of England, parts of the garden at Buckland Monachorum were limed heavily for food production; now, more than four hundred years later, there are places in the grounds that still refuse to grow any plants that thrive in acid soils.

Working the land

There has been a tendency in modern times to cast aside many of the ancient techniques, particularly those that are hard work, and to replace them with chemical or mechanical alternatives. But, fast though the motor rotary cultivator is, and effective at defoliation though herbicides may be, gardeners are now re-evaluating the old techniques, largely due to concern for the environment. There is no doubt that digging is kinder to the ground than 'rotovating', which is inclined to create a 'pan' – a layer of compacted soil below the surface – and no one can accurately predict what the long term effects of chemical usage may be.

Digging is important because it breaks up heavy soil, lets air in and allows water to drain away properly. But it is laborious. It can be backbreaking on heavy and unkind soils, or on soils in poor condition, and even on the richest

Alstroemeria Ligtu *hybrids thrive in alkaline soil but will also tolerate acid conditions.*

Well-rotted compost, seen here as a dark-coloured and friable material, helps to put life into the soil and is an essential part of good cultivation.

of loams it is very hard work. Victorians may have seen great virtue in hard graft, and in 'mortifying the flesh' thereby, but the pre-Victorian Mrs Loudon had the right attitude when she explained how to make the job as light as possible. 'The first point to be attended to, in order to render the operation of digging less laborious, is to provide a suitable spade . . . one which shall be as light as is consistent with strength, and which will penetrate the ground with the least possible trouble.' But, compared with modern implements, spades of the 1840s were cumbersome objects and it is surely not cheating to embrace the task of double digging with old-time enthusiasm, but with the aid of a stainless steel, alloy-handled spade which is light in the hand, and to which the soil won't stick! Walter P. Wright (1938) recommends that if digging is to be made easy and enjoyable, it should be tackled as follows: 'The power needed should be applied by simply letting the weight of the body depress the tool and thereby raise the load. Nor should there ever be such a thing as "lifting" with the wrist or forearm, the load should be raised by leverage, the lower hand forcing the burdened blade up,

$\mathcal{D}$OUBLE DIGGING

1. Dig a trench, one spit deep and about 60 cm (2 ft) wide, and put the soil to the back of the plot.
2. Compost, manure and soil conditioners are scattered over the surface of the lower level, ensuring an even spread. 3. Use the soil from the next trench to fill in the first and continue until the whole plot has been treated; use the soil from the first trench to fill in the last.

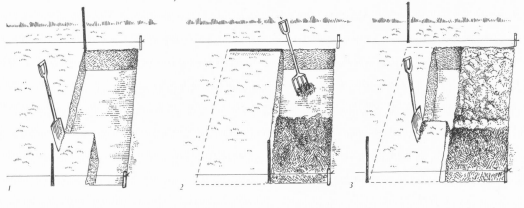

the upper hand balancing it on the flexed shoulder muscles and with a twist of the wrist turning a full "spit" and neatly over.'

Digging need not be a frequent operation. Double digging a new border, even when the soil is extra-tired and in need of much improvement, need only be carried out once. The deep trench digging where each spitful of earth is turned right over is, says Mrs Loudon, 'too laborious to be performed by anyone but a gardener's labourer.' In my view it is unnecessary. It is important, however, where you plan to dig only once in a very long while, to dig deeply enough to open up the soil and to incorporate manure or compost to a reasonable depth – 20 cm (8 in) to 25 cm (10 in) should suffice for this.

The best way to incorporate any soil improver such as compost, leafmould or manure is to spread it evenly over the surface and to dig it in as you go. You will need a layer about 5 cm (2 in) thick over the whole area to be dug in. This will ensure an even incorporation at several levels, but if the prospect of treading on stinking material does not appeal, a traditional alternative would be to lay it in the bottom of the trench. This buries all the compost or manure, but may place it a little too deep to be of optimum use to the plants. The task should be carried out in autumn.

Once the digging has been done, remaining soil care is merely a matter of avoiding compaction and keeping the structure as open as possible by occasional forking through and by repairing local damage caused by trampling or by rain falling constantly on a bare surface – nothing is better at soil-conditioning than a permanent cover of plants.

MULCHING

Mulching means to place a layer of material, such as manure, lawn mowings, leafmould or straw, on the surface of the soil around plants.

Besides mulches, such as compost, straw or manure, that can be laid on the soil, a dust-dry surface also makes a fine mulch and can be developed by repeated hoeing. Thus, good weed control also creates the mulch!

It is a practice much favoured by old-time gardeners. Mulching is beneficial in dry climates, as it helps the soil to retain moisture, but it is only effective if the mulch is applied to a damp soil. A mulch is also an excellent means of suppressing weeds. If the mulch consists of animal manure or compost, it will also supply valuable nutrients to the soil. Another form of mulch that gardeners used to rely on was the dust formed by frequent hoeing – an inexpensive mulch indeed! Mulches are usually applied in late spring or early summer.

A sixteenth-century engraving of gardeners busy at work planting out young specimens and digging the soil in preparation.

Manures and other soil improvers

Perhaps one of the most unnatural aspects of modern horticulture, and modern agriculture for that matter, has been the abandonment of organic substances and the widespread use of chemical fertilizers to replace plant foods. Phosphates, nitrates and potassium salts are acceptable and nourishing for plants whether they have come from a factory or from the dung hill or compost heap, since plants feed on simple inorganic chemicals. The difference is that manufactured mineral salts, particularly nitrates, are readily soluble and are easily washed out through the soil into the aquifers below: but when they are naturally locked into organic matter it takes more time for decomposition to release these simple chemicals, and therefore ensures a slow, steady supply of plant foods. And when nutrients are added to the soils in the form of dungs or composts, humus (see page 142) is also added.

Until the middle of the nineteenth century, it was thought that green plants could actually absorb organic matter, in the form of 'dissolved humus', through their roots. Observation showed that crops grown in humus-rich soil always fared better than those in pure mineral soils and so the assumption seemed logical. However, it is now understood that plants manufacture most of their tissue from the carbon dioxide in the atmosphere and absorb only mineral nutrients from the ground. But, for soil to perform really well, it must contain that magic mixture of organic matter, micro-organisms, water and air.

To garden successfully using traditional methods, therefore, it is necessary to prepare compost, and, if possible, to bring in manure from outside. On heavy land, however, additional soil improvers may be needed. An ancient practice was to add grit or pea gravel to open up the soil structure, and this is still beneficial. The soil can also be lightened by digging in such unlikely ingredients as bonfire ash or even road sweepings – provided these are not contaminated with previously applied herbicides of course.

ANIMAL MANURES

Manure is one of the best sources of organic matter for the garden: it will improve the texture of the soil so that plant roots can make their way deeper into the soil to find food and water and it also supplies vital nutrients.

Old gardeners would talk of manures being 'hot' or 'cold'. A hot manure is fresh animal waste which generates heat as it decomposes and which gives off ammonia vapour and is caustic to plants. Fresh horse dung is hot; so is pure poultry manure and pig muck. Cattle manure, especially when it is incorporated with plenty of straw, is less hot, because the rotting process is more sedate, and the material is consequently less caustic to plants.

Manure laid on the surface of the soil will act as a mulch while it rots down.

Only fresh dung has a use as a generator of heat (see hotbed, page 21). For soil-feeding purposes, all manures should be well rotted, and rotted manure is much easier and more pleasant to handle and to spread on the soil. This helps to minimize the number of weed seeds included in the animal waste material, and reduces the risk of burning the roots of plants. Frequently, manures that are purchased or acquired by other means are partially rotted. Horse manure should be left in a heap for at least two months – a year is better – occasionally turned, until the foetid, strawy nature of the fresh product gradually transforms to a crumbly consistency. Cow manure should be left for about a year.

COMPOST

The easiest way to build up humus, particularly if farmyard manure is difficult to acquire, is to make your own compost. This is an ancient art which, to some gardeners, becomes almost a way of life. Successful compost-makers are thrifty souls who save and hoard absolutely everything that is rottable. The reason that waste vegetation is rotted first is that the bacteria that decompose this material need nitrogen, and if you put the vegetation straight back into the soil, the bacteria will draw on the very nitrogen your garden plants need in order to survive and prosper.

Thrifty gardeners have always known that it is essential to build up the organic content of the soil. These compost bins are ideal for the purpose, being open and airy but with welded mesh sides to retain the material for composting.

> 66 *Does* some very busy (we will not say lazy) reader sigh? Had he hoped to hear that by substituting a quart of artificial manure for a load of dung he could get first-class crops merely by scratching the soil? It cannot be. 99
>
> Walter P. Wright, 1938

Lawn mowings, cut-back perennials and discarded vegetable waste can all be used to make compost. Prunings and clippings from trees and shrubs are good too, although woody prunings will need to be cut as small as you can before adding them to the compost heap; a mechanical compost shredder would be a boon here. Compost can also include organic kitchen refuse, but everything should be raw, and cut small. Do not include any diseased or infected material, pernicious weeds such as ground elder (*Aegopodium podagraria*), couch grass (*Agropyron repens*) or bindweed (*Convolvulus arvensis*), or weed seeds.

You can also add animal manure, which will supply much-needed mineral nutrients. If you can't find a supply of animal manures, then you could use seaweed meal, dried blood, or a proprietary brand compost activator (available from most garden suppliers).

Although you can just keep your compost in a heap in a corner of the garden, a compost container of some kind is useful. It gives a tidier appearance, and allows the compost to rot all the way through to the edges of the heap. However, it is important that a bin allows in plenty of air, and should be made up of wooden slats for this purpose. If you want to keep the compost in a heap, then it will need to be turned after about two months. If this isn't done, the heap will degenerate into a stinking black mess. Turning also prevents the compost from overheating at its centre by bringing unrotted material from the outside of the heap to the centre. If the heap looks dry when you turn it, it should be watered. However, it should not be allowed to stand in the rain, and should be protected by some form of open-sided shelter. In fact, it would be best to have two compost heaps, one that is left to rot down properly while the other is being filled up.

Material suitable for the compost heap include vegetable stalks, hedge clippings and lawn mowings. These can be left in a heap to rot down to make a fine friable compost, provided that the material is turned over regularly and not allowed to become either too wet or too dry.

Newly fallen leaves should be piled in a corner of the garden where they can be left to decay undisturbed. The resulting leaf mould is put back on the soil as a valuable mulch.

Whether you're making your compost in a heap or in a bin, it's best to start with a layer of bulky material such as straw (thoroughly wet it first), large weeds or horse manure (this will allow air in through the bottom). Then add a layer of, say, grass mowings mixed with twigs and damp straw. Each layer should be 15 cm (6 in) deep. Then add a layer of horse manure, or a dusting of seaweed meal or activator. Add another 15 cm (6 in) layer of material, then sprinkle with lime. Continue as described (but make sure you don't sprinkle lime on to the 'activator', whether it's manure or the ready-made kind). The heap or bin should be between 90 cm (3 ft) and 1.2 m (4 ft) high. It is vital to keep the pile well aerated, and you should make holes using a pointed stick after a few weeks, then check these regularly.

The compost is ready when it is brown and crumbly and has a wonderful sweet smell. This stage can take anything from five to six months in the winter or two months in warm weather.

Leafmould Leaves will rot down to a rich brown powdery substance, a good source of organic matter and humus. Leafmould offers a wonderful compost, but it takes anything from one to three years for it to rot down properly, so you need to find a spot in the garden where the leaves can be left undisturbed for this time. If the pile looks very dry in the summer, water it a little. If you want to speed up the process, shred the leaves first and use an activator. Don't use evergreen leaves, as they never decay properly – recommended leaves include elm, oak and beech.

Green manuring The Amish were one of the first farmers to use clover to improve the soil (clover 'fixes' nitrogen in the soil), and this is the main advantage of green manuring: to supply plant nutrients. It also provides a small amount of organic matter. Where the soil is very poor, particularly if it is very sandy or chalky, green manuring may be helpful, as generations of farmers have discovered. The best way to use green manure is to sow a winter crop in the late summer or early autumn, which can then be dug in before using the ground for cultivation in spring. For the garden, the most useful green crops are any of the legumes, such as alfalfa, lupins and broad beans, or red clover and winter tare. These all fix nitrogen in the soil. The crop should be cut just as the flowers start and should be left to wilt on the surface of the soil for a few days before being dug into the top soil. Non-nitrogen-fixing plants that can be used for green manuring include buckwheat, rye and mustard (but don't use mustard on a patch where you have just grown anything from the cabbage family).

Traditional hints on cultivation techniques

Although the main gardening techniques have been covered in some detail elsewhere, there remain a number of old-fashioned practices that have such a useful application in our modern day, environmentally friendly gardens that it would be wrong not to mention them.

Below right: old-fashioned varieties of peas need support from pea sticks. Early twentieth-century flower gardeners adopted this system to support lax perennials in their newly fashionable herbaceous borders.

Below: metal hoop stakes were favoured by Edwardian gardeners and are still being manufactured by specialist firms. They are easy to use and soon vanish among the growing vegetation.

PLANT SUPPORT

The mixed shrub and herbaceous borders which are so popular today depend for their success on a naturalistic, informal feel. Obvious plant supports such as canes and string can spoil the effect, but without support many of the old-fashioned herbaceous perennials would collapse. A favourite system used by many nineteenth- and early twentieth-century gardeners was to support perennials by pushing twiggy branches, often of birch, into the ground around the plants. This form of support also works very well with annuals, especially those with lax stems. When they are visible, at the beginning of the season, these natural supports do not look unsightly, and by mid-summer they will have disappeared behind all the plant growth anyway.

Supporting climbers on walls, especially in the Victorian kitchen garden, was an art in itself. Vine eyes – spikes with a hole at the blunt end through which support wires could be threaded – were invented to support grape

Opposite: in areas where wind is a problem, tall vegetables such as broccoli and, here, Brussels sprouts can be staked to avoid wind-rock and distress to the roots.

vines in hothouses but are a universal necessity for all wall culture. Installed with stout wires running horizontally along the wall, they enable a heavy weight of mixed plant material to be securely supported.

In *The English Flower Garden* (1883) William Robinson warmly approves of the concept of growing a climbing plant through a host tree or bush. Delicate climbers, he says, 'Deserve to be used in rather a new way ... namely for throwing a delicate lacework of flowers over the evergreen and other choice shrubs grown in our gardens.' The flame nasturtium (*Tropaeolum speciosum*), he suggests, is especially useful in this respect and he also recommends clematis for the same purpose. Nowadays, it is more common to allow all kinds of trailing plants to drape themselves about in the mixed border, but we should heed Robinson's warning not to allow vigorous climbers to swamp their neighbours or their hosts.

SPECIAL CARE FOR WINTER

Plant collectors bombarded a keen gardening public with so many new introductions in the nineteenth century that it must have been difficult to learn about such important details as soil preferences, planting aspect and, above all, winter hardiness. We all love to grow plants whose natural climatic preferences fail, just, to match up with what our winters offer! A series of means of affording winter protection have therefore evolved, particularly for those who garden in a cold area where winter frost or, worse, excessive winter wet take their toll.

Many of the old gardeners packed susceptible plants in straw, *in situ*, during the coldest months. In the sixteenth century even fruit trees were lagged with straw during winter and kept in wraps until the blossom was nearly ready to burst in spring. This is a little extreme, but many marginally hardy plants benefit from a bulky, dry, winter mulch of leafmould, straw

Old-fashioned herbaceous borders need regular attention, not only by keeping weeds down but also by supporting tall plants and removing dead or dying material from time to time.

or dry fern closely packed over their roots to minimize frost damage.

A simpler approach to protect vulnerable roots, if dried bracken fern is hard to come by in your area or if you dislike the prospect of straw blowing about the garden, is to cut off small branches of a conifer – the Leyland cypress is good for this, because it regenerates so swiftly – and push these into the ground like a windbreak all round the plant.

As a safety precaution, such tender plants as pelargoniums, fuchsias, perennial salvias and so on should have cuttings taken in late summer and, once rooted, these should be overwintered indoors or in a greenhouse. Many of them make attractive windowsill plants for winter anyway – an attribute also recognized by eighteenth- and nineteenth-century folk.

PERENNIAL MAINTENANCE

Perennials in the traditional herbaceous border would be lifted and divided at least every second year. This total replanting approach was fine for households which employed full-time gardeners, but for most modern situations is too much like hard work. There is a perfectly sound compromise, however, blending the old with the new: simply divide plants on a piecemeal basis as and when they need it. Working through the border in autumn, it will be easy to spot those plants which will benefit from division and those that can happily be left for at least another season. Plants whose roots are congested begin to die in the middle and lose vigour, so these are the ones to divide.

Weed control

Preventing plants from setting seeds has always been recognized as being crucial to effective weed control. Spotting weed problems early saves much bother as does growing good, dense ground-cover plants to inhibit weed growth.

> *ONE YEAR'S SEED IS TEN YEARS' WEED.*
>
> Traditional saying

Mulches (see page 146), too, are helpful in reducing the number of germinating weed seedlings, as well as helping to reduce moisture loss from the soil surface. E.T. Cook, in *Gardening for Beginners* at the turn of the century, writes: 'The gardener, whenever he can, places about . . . garden crops or fruit trees, a layer of manure containing a good proportion of straw; or failing that, cocoa-nut fibre refuse or decayed leaves, as these catch the sun's rays and protect the soil, thus keeping moisture in it.' (It is interesting to note that coconut fibre is mentioned but not peat.)

As far as 'chemical' methods are concerned, one of the earliest known weed killers was salt. This was sprinkled on gravel paths, as prevention rather than cure, but it was still pretty hit and miss. The important thing was not to water the area until the weeds had died. Probably more effective is to mix up a solution of salt and boiling water and pour this over the weeds, and, for gravel areas, to mix together a solution of salt, ashes and tobacco in water.

Pests and diseases

One big advantage we have over our forebears is technology. We can zap weeds or bugs at a stroke with chemical sprays; we can control fungal diseases with efficient fungicides; we can breed flowers and produce at an accelerated rate to come up with varieties that look better and better and that will sit on a supermarket shelf for days on end without deteriorating. Now we are even into genetic engineering and soon we will be producing all kinds of freakish monsters and cross-breeds which have highly developed qualities of one sort or another.

Many gardens now feature tender plants that need some form of protection during the winter, but it is perfectly possible, as here, to create a garden that looks attractive in winter and summer without needing a great deal of additional care during the colder months.

Aphid brush

Sulphurator for spraying sulphur on plants

Read's water syringe

But just how precious are these advantages? Were Loudon's strawberries inferior to the delectable-looking but utterly tasteless objects that we find being retailed today? Were the Empress Josephine's roses in her famous garden at Malmaison any less lovely for the mildew they undoubtedly carried than modern roses, which depend on regular spraying to keep them spotlessly clean?

It would be foolish to say that all modern aspects of gardening are bad and all the old ways good, but, when one looks at flavour, most of the old food crop varieties have the edge. As far as pest and disease control is concerned, we may have the technology, but our ancestors were much more observant, and much more meticulous, in their plant care. Since they could not resort to the sprayer, they had to recognize pest problems *before* they had time to proliferate. They would observe, for instance, that such roses as 'Zéphirene Drouhin' were vulnerable to disease and would therefore avoid the mistake of planting them in a place susceptible to mildew such as a warm wall, facing west. They would be familiar, especially after the horrific Irish famine of the 1840s, with the dangers of blight, and would clear every scrap of straw residue away after

Young vegetables are especially vulnerable in some areas to being attacked by birds. Wire cages give the vegetables extra protection until they have fully developed their root systems.

harvesting their potatoes in the vegetable garden. In short, they soon learned that hygiene and discipline were the key.

Today's successful organic gardeners, shunning many aspects of modern technology as they do, are therefore the people who have the most in common with our forebears. They are closely in tune with their plants and they know that the most important skill they must develop is the ability to act as soon as anything begins to go amiss.

Slugs, snails and other insects To obtain a delightfully balanced view, I turn yet again to Mrs Loudon (1846) who begins her section on insect pests thus: 'Insects and snails and slugs are the terror of all gardeners; and the destruction they effect in some seasons, in small gardens, is almost beyond the bounds of credibility.' She goes on to explain how beneficial song birds are in eating pests, extolling the virtues of an equilibrium between the welfare of her garden plants and of friendly wildlife.

Later, she does mention chemical control. Tobacco, she suggests, is an efficacious insecticide, either blown as smoke over caterpillars and other insects or in the form of tobacco water, made 'by steeping half a pound of the best tobacco in a gallon of hot water'. Once the mixture had cooled, pest-infested shoots could be dipped into it and then rinsed in clean water almost immediately afterwards to prevent the tobacco from damaging the plant tissue. And that was about as far as her repertoire of chemical controls went.

Aphids For aphids on roses, Mrs Loudon preferred to use the simpler method of dipping whole branches into bowls of water and shaking them gently so that they floated off. Other old-time gardeners used specially designed soft brushes, but, whichever way you looked at it, eradication techniques were time-consuming and managing the garden to minimize the incidence of pests was the key to success.

Birds On the whole, birds are very useful in the garden, but they become a menace when it comes to seedling crops and ripening fruits. In a fairly small area, they can be prevented from eating seeds if you place sticks in the bed and draw dark thread tightly between them. The same can be done on fruit trees and bushes, using the branches to tie on the thread. Rather than risk being entangled in the threads, birds will prefer to land elsewhere.

Wasps In 1762 Gilbert White recommended trapping wasps by hanging up bottles containing treacle and beer among his grapes 'which make a great havock among them'. The same method can be applied to fruit trees, but it would be more effective to put the mixture in jars and cover them with paper lids which have a hole in the centre – the wasps will be able to get in but not out and will drown in the beer.

A well-balanced, wildlife-friendly garden will provide the right habitat for a wide range of insects, including hover flies, ladybirds and centipedes, all of which feed on aphids and other insect pests. Growing plants as healthily as possible, ensuring that the soil is in optimum condition, and generally maximizing fertility are important ways of stacking up the odds against pests and diseases. If a catholic mixture of plants is organized in the ground so that each one is able to grow to its optimum size without either overcrowding or undue isolation, the chances of problems are considerably reduced and the whole garden will look cared for and well managed. It is all a question of creating a balanced habitat. The knowledge and understanding of that balance seems to have been held by generations of gardeners – that is, except the present one!

In the depths of winter, when greenstuff is hard to find, pigeons and other foraging birds will often raid a kitchen garden. The old-fashioned cure for this was to employ an apprentice to wander among the crops all through the day. In modern times a plastic net is a less laborious alternative!

Bibliography

Acton, Eliza, *Modern Cookery for Private Families*, 1845

Annals of Horticulture, 1846

Bacon, Francis, *Of Gardens*, 1625

Beeton, Mrs, *The Book of Household Management*, 1861

Boland, Bridget and Maureen, *Old Wive's Lore for Gardeners*. London: The Bodley Head, 1976

Cook, E.T., *Gardening for Beginners*

Gentil, Francis, *Le Jardinier Solitaire*, 1706

Gerard, John, *Herball*, 1633

Gore and Fleming, *The English Garden*. London: Michael Joseph, 1979

Hamilton, Geoff, *Successful Organic Gardening*. London: Dorling Kindersley, 1987

Hamilton, Geoff, *The Ornamental Kitchen Garden*. London: BBC Books, 1990

Hartley, Dorothy, *Food in England*. London: Macdonald, 1954

Hellyer, Arthur, *The Illustrated Encyclopedia of Gardening*. London: Marks and Spencer, 1986

Hill, Thomas, *The Gardener's Labyrinth*, originally published in 1577 and reprinted a number of times. Most quotes taken from the 1652 edition, with thanks to Oxford University Press, 1987.

Hole, Dean Reynolds, *Our Gardens*, 1899

Jekyll, Gertrude, *Colour in the Flower Garden*, 1908

Jekyll, Gertrude, and Weaver, Sir Lawrence, *Gardens for Small Country Houses*, 1912

Leighton, Ann, *Early American Gardens*. Amherst: The University of Massachusetts Press, 1986

Leighton, Ann, *American Gardens in the Eighteenth Century*. Amherst: The University of

Massachusetts Press, 1986

Loudon, John Claudius, *Encyclopedia of Gardening*, 1822

Loudon, John Claudius, *Gardener's Magazine*

Loudon, Mrs, *Gardening for Ladies*, 1846

Loewenfeld, Claire and Buck, Philippa, *The Complete Book of Herbs and Spices*. London: David and Charles, 1974

Parkinson, John, *Paradisi in Sole, Paradus Terrestris*, 1629

Robinson, William, *The English Flower Garden*. London: John Murray, 1883

Robinson, William, *The Wild Garden*, 1894

Rose, G., *The Traditional Garden Book*. London: Dorling Kindersley, 1989

Sanecki, Kay N., *Old Garden Tools*. Shire, 1987

Schofield, Bernard, *A Miscellany of Garden Wisdom*, London: Collins, 1991

Switzer, Stephen, *The Practical Fruit-Gardener*, 1752

Thomas, G.S., *The Old Shrub Roses*. London: Dent, 1957

Thompson, Robert, *The Gardener's Assistant*, 1859

Twain, Mark, *Pudd'nhead Wilson*, 1894

Toogood, Alan, *Propagation*. London, Dent

Tusser, Thomas, *Five Hundred Points of Good Husbandry*, 1557

Verey, Rosemary, *Classic Garden Design*. London: John Murray, 1984

Wright, Walter P., *Scientific & Practical Gardening for School and Home*. London: George Allen and Unwin, first published in 1928; third edition, 1938

Index

Foxgloves in an old-fashioned wild garden.

A Colonial herb garden in the Van Dyke style with traditional raised beds.

A basket of summer flowers, including Agastache, *alliums, and nasturtiums.*

ACKNOWLEDGEMENTS

Photographer's Acknowledgements

I would like to thank everybody who has allowed me to photograph their garden for this book: Mr Ablett, Roy Balaam, Faith and Karl Balaam, Alix Blomer, Mr and Mrs Peter Carver, Mr de Giorgio, Tony and Kay Diment, Mrs Gordon Foster, Betty Gloster, The Hon. Mrs Peter Healing, Mr and Mrs Huntington, Mrs Innes, Dr and Mrs O. James, Kirsten Jones, Jan Joyce, Anne and Robert Niven, Mrs Pickard, Mr and Mrs Paul Picton, Jenny Raworth, Jill Richardson, Mr and Mrs P. Stockitt, The Rev. Henry Thorold, Lord and Lady Tollemache, Rosemary Verey, Mr Hugh Murray Wells, Mr and Mrs Westerdale and Hamish Wright. Thanks to Mr and Mrs Fry for the photograph on page 112, taken at Fulbeck Hall, Fulbeck, Lincolnshire, England. For information on opening times, garden seminars, etc., contact Mrs M. Fry at Fulbeck Hall. Tel: 0400-72205. I would also like to give a special thanks to Robert Jones for finding all the old garden tools and implements which have been photographed for the book; Giles Stokoe for assisting, and David Robertson for his invaluable support.

Publishers' Acknowledgements

The Publishers would like to give a special thanks to **DEREK FELL** for reading the text and for supplying the photographs on the following pages: 1, 3, 8 bottom, 14, 16 top, 17, 23, 29, 30, 48 bottom, 53, 55 bottom, 58, 59, 60, 67 top, 85 top, 91 bottom, 94, 96 bottom, 103 bottom, 106, 109, 122, 148, 157, 158, 159

The Publishers would also like to thank the following for supplying additional pictures:
Hugh Palmer: pages 14 bottom, 16 bottom, 90, 91 top, 93, 99, 100, 102, 109, 113 bottom, 116, 139, 149 bottom, 150 below right.
Lucy Mason: pages 6 top, 27 left, 30, 73 bottom, 81, 92, 118 top, 123, 140, 149 top.

All other photographs by **Jacqui Hurst**.

Picture: *a detail from a formal flower garden.*